DATE DUE

~~DE 9 '02~~			
~~OC 3 1 '08~~			

Women in Kuwait

In memory of my brother, Mughni Abdul al-Mughni
(1957–1978)

R

Women in Kuwait

The Politics of Gender

Haya al-Mughni

Saqi Books

British Library Cataloguing-in-Publication Data
A catalogue record for this book is available from the British Library

ISBN 0 86356 199 3

First published 1993 by
Saqi Books
26 Westbourne Grove
London W2 5RH

Typeset by Group E, London

Contents

Abbreviations

AFO	Arab Family Organization
AFU	Arab Feminist Union
AWDS	Arab Women's Development Society
CSS	Cultural and Social Society
EPS	Environmental Protection Society
KD	Kuwaiti dinar(s)
ICS	Islamic Care Society
KNUS	Kuwait National Union of Students
KWU	Kuwaiti Women's Union
UN	United Nations
WCSS	Women's Cultural and Social Society

Glossary

abbaya	women's long black cloak, worn over the dress and covering the entire body
adab	good manners
adab al-mar'a	women's good manners
aib	shameful
al-amal al-salih	virtuous deed(s)
amir	prince; ruler
anashid [pl.]	mystical songs
asala	authenticity
ashira	group of families
asil	pure origin; noble descent
asl	genealogy; line of descent
aura	sexual
awqaf	religious endowments
aya	verse of the Quran
baharna	people of Bahraini origin
baisari	non-noble origins
batin	esoteric
bedoun [pl.]	stateless citizens
bint	daughter
boshiya	thick black face covering for women
busata' [pl.]	simple
da'wa	mission; preaching
da'iya	preacher
dhikr	invocation of God
dira	territorial unit
dishdasha	men's traditional garment
diwaniya	men's reception room; [by extension] social gathering
du'a	invocation of God
farij	neighbourhood
farrasha	attendant
fatwa	legal ruling
figh	Islamic jurisprudence

fitna	disorder, chaos; also associated with a dangerously attractive woman
gabila	tribe
hadith	sayings of the Prophet Muhammad
hajj	pilgrimage to Mecca
hakim	ruler
hamula	husband's family
haram	forbidden, taboo; shame
hijab	women's veil, consisting of a headcover
ihsan	good deed(s)
imam	mosque preacher
iman	faith
istighfar	seeking God's forgiveness
jadwal al-ibada	worship chart
jama'a	group, community, assembly; companionship
jihad	holy war
jinn	demon(s)
jism	body
karama	honour
khataba	marriage broker
khelwa	[for a woman] being alone with men
khutba	sermon
kufur	religious infidelity
kut	fortress
mahr	dowry
majlis	tribal council
mar'a	woman
ma'rifa	knowledge
mawlad al-nabi	birth of the Prophet
muassisin	founders
muharam	male relative
mujtama'	community
mullah	preacher
muntada	religious gathering; religious seminar
muntasibin	affiliated [members]
murid	student (in a Sufi order)
murshid [fem. *murshida*]	teacher (in a Sufi order)
mutawa'a	religious instructor
nafs	soul; self
nahda	rebirth, progress, awakening

nawafil	additional prayers
nukhoda	ship's captain
rab'	friends and kin who form a cohesive social network
rajiya	backwardness
al-rasul	the Messenger (the Prophet Muhammad)
ruh	spirit
salaf	loan payments
salat	official Islamic prayer ritual
salik	member, student (of Sufi order); spiritual seeker
sawm	fasting
sharaf	honour
sharifa	respectable
sheikh	spiritual leader
sheikh masheyikh	sheikh of sheikhs
sheikha [fem.]	spiritual healer
shura	consultation
sifat [pl.]	qualities, attributes, features
sifat al-mar'a	female qualities
sirat al-nabi	life of the Prophet
sufur	(state of being) unveiled
sum'a	reputation
sunnah	words and deeds of the Prophet Muhammad
suq	market
suq khairi	charity bazaar
tabaq al-khair	'the bowl of charity'
tabaruj	adornment; display of feminine charms
taqaddum	progress
tariqa	spiritual/mystical path
tasawwuf	Islamic spirituality/mysticism
tawakkul	absolute dependence on God
tawawish	pearl merchants
tawhid	union with God
tawjid	reading the Quran
tazkiyat al-nafs	self-purification; purification of the soul
tujjar	merchants
turath	cultural heritage
ulama	religious scholars
umm	mother
umma	Islamic community/nation/people

usra	family, household
al-usra al-wahida	one family
uzuba	celibacy
wasat	in the middle
watan	homeland, native country
zakat	Muslim religious tax of 2.5 per cent on capital and earnings
zar	spirit; spiritual possession
zauja	wife
zayy al-islami	Islamic costume consisting of a loose dress and a headcover that hide the woman's body except for her face and hands
zina	adultery
ziyarat	paying social visits

Preface and Acknowledgements

My first contact with the women's organizations in Kuwait dates back to 1984 when I went searching for answers to and support for my personal problems. I was then angry and confused. In my job, no matter how hard I worked, I could not expect to be promoted or rewarded as my male colleagues were. Being a woman meant that I had to be obedient and pleasing, and give up my personal needs in order to earn the respect of men and of the society at large. It meant that I had to comply, both at home and at work, with male authority.

The women's organizations were then very busy trying to secure suffrage for women. I tried to help but did not have enough energy and enthusiasm. Nor was I entirely convinced that political rights were the main issue for women in Kuwait. I felt that far more pressing problems needed to be tackled, problems that lay at the heart of the relationships between men and women in this society. I felt disappointed with the women's organizations without fully knowing why.

Thus I am indebted to all those who introduced me to feminism and supported me through my studies. Najat Sultan introduced me to the feminist movement, sharing with me her thoughts and ideas on feminism. Colette Dowling's *The Cinderella Complex*[1] was my first reading in feminism: it changed my life. In October 1985 I moved to England to pursue my academic career in women's studies, and eventually made the women's organizations in Kuwait the subject of my research. These organizations are still very active in Kuwait. The Iraqi occupation interrupted their activities for seven months but did not change the essence of their work.

I owe a great deal to my friends and colleagues at Exeter University for their emotional and intellectual support throughout the period of my studies. I should like to thank John Vincent, Barry Turner, Helen Kay, Julian Coker, Jock Mickshik, and Sue and Stuart Dawson. I am grateful, too, for the insightful comments, suggestions and editing of Helen Snively. I remain deeply indebted to André Gaspard and to all the people of Saqi Books for their support and encouragement. Without their help this book would not have been published.

Last, but not least, my family deserve the warmest gratitude and acknowledgement for encouraging me to write even though they do not share my beliefs and convictions.

Introduction

Interest in Middle Eastern women emerged long before the present rising tide of religious movements in the Muslim world. A century ago, the condition of Arab women, veiled and secluded behind mud walls, attracted the attention of Western travellers who were both appalled and fascinated by the way women were treated. These early observers fostered the belief that Muslim women have no control within their societies and that their lives are entirely shaped and dictated by customs and Islamic norms embodied in their own cultures.

Until recently, few scholars questioned this belief. In much of the literature on the Middle East two inaccurate images prevail: first, that women have no freedom in their most crucial life decisions; and, second, that women's subordinate position can be attributed to the power of Islam rather than to economic, patriarchal and political forces. Middle Eastern women are often treated as a homogeneous category, with little attention to the ways in which class, geography and politics influence their individual experiences.

This book proposes an alternative view: that Middle Eastern women are responsible for their own oppression. I look at upper-class Kuwaiti women and their organizations to show that their loyalties are primarily to their families and kin, and that they act in ways which actually reinforce rather than challenge female subordination.

In Middle Eastern societies, kinship remains a central principle of social, political and economic organization. Western penetration in the mid-nineteenth century did not entail a weakening of family ties and obligations, or a reduction of marriages between kin, or a diminution of husbands' authority over wives and children. The Arab family withstood the forces of change and held on to its patriarchal and authoritarian character. Even today, a man's rights over his wife and children are quasi-absolute. Family members continue 'to live in the same neighborhood, to inter-marry, to group on a kinship basis, and to expect a great deal from one another'.[1]

Familial roles form the basis of social identification. A married man is often called not by his own name but by that of his son; thus Abu Ali is the father of Ali. Women are also exclusively defined in terms of their being someone's *umm* (mother), *zauja* (wife) or *bint* (daughter). It is not socially acceptable for a woman to lead a celibate life. Unmarried women are pitied and made to feel social failures, having to live with their own families and with no children of their own. Virginity is still the norm until marriage. A woman who loses her virginity not only brings shame on her own family, but also loses her chance of finding a suitable Arab husband. In Kuwait, as in many other Arab countries, adultery and other instances of sexual intercourse outside marriage are listed in the penal code as crimes against public decency, leading to a prison sentence of up to five years.

The social obligations and norms that regulate women's lives do not necessarily mean that all women have similar experiences. Access to resources and privileges, which are mediated by kinship and class relations, divide women and set them apart. By virtue of their class membership, upper-class women have much wider opportunities than others. In Kuwait, women occupy posts such as ministry under-secretaries and deans of university colleges, but these are mainly the privilege of women from the ruling elite and the merchant class. Research into the relationship between female employment and class in Turkey has revealed an important and disturbing fact: the education of women and their access to prestigious professions are not so much a means for mobility as for class consolidation. Educated upper-class women pose less of a threat than upwardly mobile men from modest backgrounds; their recruitment allows the elite to fill vacancies caused by a shortage of qualifed upper-class men.[2]

The role played by Arab women in class politics has not been studied adequately. Scholars have been more concerned to pinpoint the constraints that circumscribe women's lives than to look at how women influence the political directions taken by their societies. Kinship relations form the basis of these societies. Both the economy and the political system are usually run and controlled by groups of families, known collectively as the *ashira*. In Kuwait, political decisions are still taken in *diwaniyas*, men's social gatherings adapted from the pre-oil era. The *diwaniya* is confined to male heads of families and other men from a similar social background, forming a society which operates for its own collective benefit.[3] It functions as a male institution in which family decisions are made, business is conducted and political issues are discussed. It is the interpenetration of kinship with the economic and political organization that gives Kuwaiti women a crucial role in class politics. Women are the producers and mediators of kinship relations, and form the core of the alliances within and between families which maintain class cohesion.

Upper-class women engage in a network of public and semi-public activities that are central to class organization, and are as vital and significant as the men's *diwaniyas*. The most important of these activities are *ziyarat* (paying social visits), arranged marriages and female association. A study of 526 heads of households in Kuwait found a strong relationship between the immediate family and the kin network, particularly among the upper strata: 80 per cent of respondents visit their kin daily or weekly and 48 per cent are married to relatives, of whom 79 per cent are first cousins. Business relationships within families are relatively strong: more than half of the respondents had relatives in the workplace or as business partners.[4]

Visiting is not confined to the kin network; it also involves families of a similar social standing. In this social exchange process, women discuss and make arrangements for their children's future marriages. Marriage can only take place within the same lineage or between families in a similar social position with respect to prestige, power and privilege. The daughters of wealthy merchant families, for example, are not allowed to marry men outside their class boundaries. The first generation of educated Kuwaiti women, whose families refused to marry them off to men whom they considered to be of lower social status, paid a heavy price in this society, ending up as spinsters.[5] The preference that young upper-class women show nowadays for marrying within their own stratum is not entirely related to the fear of spinsterhood; they also feel the pressure to preserve their class in the face of the social and political disturbances taking place in the region.

Of all Kuwaiti women, those of the elite and the merchant class have been the most eager to preserve the kin relations from which they gain prestige and access to many privileges. Their loyalty to their own class has often superseded their loyalty to members of their own sex. Women's associations have been established to serve the interests of their social stratum rather than the interests of all women. These organizations, which seem to operate as recreational centres for women to meet, kill time and voice some feminist concerns, provide an important instrument through which the ruling elite can exercise control over women and monitor their lives.

This book examines the political role of women's organizations in Kuwait and shows how women's class position has affected their actions. It also shows how upper-class women have very little interest in promoting feminist issues and how they neglect, to the extent of denying, the many problems Kuwaiti women face in a society exclusively controlled by men. The Kuwaiti elite still has a crucial interest in controlling female sexuality, promulgating laws on morality, and defending the family and the traditional role of women within it.

My analysis is framed by three concepts: class, patriarchy and gender. I do not use the concept of class in a Marxist sense; I refer, rather, to a more sociological understanding of class which draws on Weber's concept of status: a set of persons who stand in similar positions with respect to some form of power, privilege or prestige. I use the term patriarchy to refer to the institutionalized system of male dominance which finds its expression in the family and in the society at large. The concept of gender refers to the socially constructed aspect of femininity and masculinity. Motherhood is often construed as a central element of femininity. In this line of thinking, women's responsibility for childcare is justified by their ability to bear and nurse children.

Chapter 1 looks at the historical process of class formation and the development of voluntary associations, going back to the early eighteenth century when the town of Kuwait was first established. My focus is on how the ruling elite and the merchant community came to be a powerful class, how they managed to retain their power, wealth and status in post-oil Kuwait, and on the circumstances which led to the formation of voluntary associations. Chapter 2 focuses on the lives and experiences of Kuwaiti women, guided by several questions: Did women share similar experiences during the pre-oil era? How did class and patriarchy affect their lives, and how did they experience the changes brought about by the emergence of the welfare state? Chapter 3 explores the women's organizations which emerged in the 1960s, looking at the social background of the members, their activities and the impact they had on a male-dominated society. Chapters 4 and 5 examine the contemporary women's societies, focusing on their class composition, their activities, their organizational structure, their views on women's issues and their relationships with the government. The Conclusion reviews the major findings and asks whether there is a possibility for a female solidarity to emerge in Kuwait, one that aims to defend the needs and interests of all women.

The Fieldwork Problem: Facing Suspicion as a Researcher

This book is the result of my research into Kuwaiti women's groups, based on a large number of interviews and written sources. In the winter of 1986–87 I interviewed government officials and women who were involved in the early women's organizations. The Ministry of Social Affairs and Labour made people and documents available to me, as did the main public library, al-Mubarakiya, which contains numerous historical documents, including all the early feminist journals and magazines published in Kuwait in the 1950s. In the winter of 1987–88 I worked closely with the four women's organizations that are the focus of the present study: Bayader al-Salam, the Islamic Care Society, the Girls Club and the Women's Cultural and Social Society. In this way, I was able to observe the members in their daily activities, including the kind of language they used with each other, and could experience their daily routine. I interviewed all the officers, and 20 members from each organization. I also visited all 54 voluntary organizations in Kuwait to gather data on their members and activities.

At first, I thought that my being a woman was enough to allow me access to the women's groups and to establish a warm dialogue with their members. I did not anticipate the problems that my role as a researcher would create for the fieldwork: resistance, suspicion and limited access to data. Some members simply refused to be interviewed; others showed enormous enthusiasm for the project but would not speak about their personal experiences. At all times, I was perceived as a researcher, a role which was often associated with spying. The longer I spent within each organization, the more often I heard hints of exasperation as people asked me when I was going to finish and leave. I felt like an intruder.

I began to be aware of the women's mistrust of outsiders. I was not a member, therefore I could not be trusted: I might say something to harm their *sum'a* (reputation). Kuwaiti women are always careful about what they say and how they express themselves. The male society puts so much pressure on them that they feel obliged to be secretive, presenting a good image of themselves so as to preserve their honour. There was another reason for this mistrust: my being a feminist. Although the women's societies are meant to be for all women, only a small number actually participate. The leaders did not want to be seen as not doing enough to attract more members; hence they felt threatened by my role as an observer and wanted me to leave as quickly as possible. My experience made me realize that the endless blame the societies' leaders place on Kuwaiti women for their lack of interest in women's organizations is only a cover-up for their exclusionary tactics. Although these groups were organized in the name of women, they actually serve interests other than those of women.

I had to think of alternative strategies to gain access to data, such as interviewing ex-members, finding other informants and gaining the trust and sympathy of the secretaries, who were well-informed about what was going on in each society. The familiarity and complicity that developed between the secretaries and myself enabled me to gain access to valuable documents that I could not have obtained in any other way. I was also very fortunate to meet an ex-member of Bayader al-Salam who provided me with valuable insights into the organization.

1
Class and Politics in Kuwait: some Historical Background

As late as 1950 Kuwait was a tiny sheikhdom, its population a mixture of settled people and nomads, and its economy based on trade, boat-building and pearling. With the advent of the oil-based economy, the traditional industries declined dramatically, paving the way for a new economic era. Despite the drastic economic changes, many features of the traditional tribal organization, such as the kinship system and the emphasis on patrilineal descent, continued to be firmly entrenched. Thus an examination of the basic structures of bedouin society will reveal a great deal about the functioning of contemporary Kuwaiti society.

This chapter first sets the historical stage by examining the nomadic mode of organization which existed in Central Arabia before the rise of the mercantile economy towards the beginning of the eighteenth century. It then focuses on the rise of Kuwait in 1752 and the economic and political organizations which emerged prior to the establishment of the British protectorate in 1899, the impact of British involvement in the affairs of Kuwait, and the discovery of oil and the emergence of the welfare state.

The main objectives here are to trace how the merchant families emerged as a powerful class and how the voluntary organizations developed in Kuwait. Most of the leaders of the women's organizations are members of this class, which controls the country's largest financial and commercial institutions. Historically, the present ruling family (the Al Sabah) and the merchants were the first to settle in the small town of Kuwait, transforming it into a flourishing commercial port. While the Al Sabah ruled, the merchants and their crews sailed and traded along the coasts of the Indian Ocean. The relationship between merchants and rulers was not without conflict. History records violent clashes and popular protests. I have chosen to describe these disturbances because they are important to our understanding of how the voluntary associations evolved from loose, informal clubs and societies into formal organizations with an elected board, a written constitution and a paid membership.

The Tribes of the Northern Peninsula

Until the eighteenth century, the northern part of the Arabian peninsula was fairly isolated and pastoral. Neither the desert nor the shallow coasts of the Arabian Gulf provided the bedouin with any alternative to pastoralism. In contrast, the southern part of the peninsula, with its fertile lands and more navigable sea coasts, offered an opportunity for the bedouin to engage in agriculture and maritime trade. While the southern communities enjoyed some form of prosperity, the northern nomads were still wandering 'from oasis to oasis with no further thought than surviving one more rainless summer'.[1]

The northern nomads subsisted on the proceeds of their animal stocks (camels and herds) and occasionally some caravan trade.[2] Water was very scarce and yet so vital that a complex kinship system of organization was instituted in order to limit warfare and competition over the grazing areas. In this system, the tribe owned pastures and desert wells. Each tribe had the right to its own *dira* (territorial unit) which other tribes could graze only with permission. The tribal *dira*, which could extend as much as 300 kilometres in any direction, was not a strictly bounded and exclusively occupied territory, but rather an area in which the permanent wells and oases customarily belonged to a specific tribe.[3]

Generally known as a *gabila*, a tribe consisted of groups of families (*ashira*) that were patrilineally related and had a common ancestor. Each *ashira* usually camped together in the tribal *dira* and shared the duties of herding. At the head of each *ashira* was a sheikh chosen by the *majlis* (tribal council) and at the head of the tribe stood the primary sheikh, usually referred to as *sheikh masheyikh* (sheikh of sheikhs).[4] The tribal leaders did not enjoy absolute authority over their kin groups; the term sheikh traditionally signified a wise elder and not a ruler *per se.*[5] The sheikhs were elected by the *majlis* to supervise the affairs of the *ashira*, that is, to co-ordinate the different segments of the tribe and to communicate decisions in matters such as migration, raids, war and other related economic activities. Kinsmen were consulted and had their say in major decisions. The concept of *shura* (consultation) was an important component of tribal political organization.

In the desert, *asl* (genealogy) was the central principle of social stratification. Most power was wielded by the camel-herding tribes, who claimed to have a purer and longer genealogy as descendants of the noble (*asil*) tribes of Arabia. The tribes considered to have less defined genealogical roots, such as the tribes of shepherds and blacksmiths, were positioned at the bottom of the desert social scale.

This social stratification was based on the nomadic mode of economic organization. In the desert, camels were a source of wealth and power, allowing the nomads to cover and control large areas. Thus noble tribes tended to be camel-herders, while tribes of shepherds were less mobile as they relied primarily on sheep and goats.

In order to preserve their noble origins and maintain their supremacy in the desert, the noble tribes observed a close endogamy. In his study of the tribes of northern Arabia, Harold Dickson noted:

> no Arab of a superior, or *sharif,* tribe can take a daughter from (or give a daughter to) an inferior one. Should a badawin elope with and marry a slave or a girl of inferior tribe, he can never again return to his kin, for to marry down is to defile the tribe's blood and they will kill him.[6]

Relations between tribes were marked by shifting alliances and mutual hostility. As alliances changed, certain powerful tribes were weakened and divided, while other weak tribes were absorbed into stronger ones: 'the prevalence of feuding, which served different social functions, was a major factor in preventing the emergence of a unified political entity in the northern deserts'.[7] Each nomadic tribe remained an independent political unit and its influence rarely went beyond the precarious limits of its *dira*.

The Settlement of the Bani Utub and the Rise of Kuwait

Early in the eighteenth century, structural changes began to occur in Kuwait, caused by a complex of factors. Particularly important was the revival of European mercantilism and its penetration into the northern part of the Arabian Gulf, which led many tribes and/or segments of tribes to settle along the coast and establish trading centres. Among these settlers was a group of families known as the Bani Utub (the emigrants).

According to Kuwaiti historians,[8] the Bani Utub belonged to the Aniza, a powerful noble tribe, but were expelled from their tribal *dira* following intra-tribal conflict some time in the seventeenth century. They sought refuge first in Qatar, where they spent almost 50 years. When their relationship with the ruler of Qatar began to deteriorate, the Bani Utub moved north. They settled temporarily at Mahraq in Bahrain, then near Khor al-Sabiya in the southern part of Basra before establishing themselves in the territory of the Bani Khalid, one of the most powerful tribes controlling the north-eastern part of Arabia. The ruler of the Bani Khalid had built a small *kut* (fortress) to store food and ammunition. It was around the *kut*, from which the name Kuwait derived, that the Bani Utub settled.

The Bani Utub soon formed a cordial relationship with the ruler of the Bani Khalid and were then able to achieve some measure of independence from their host. The Bani Khalid's power over the north-eastern part of Arabia gradually weakened as a result of two factors: disputes between family members over the management of the sheikhdom and the growing power of the Wahhabis in Central Arabia. By 1752 the Bani Utub had complete control over Kuwait. Sabah bin Jabir was elected as sheikh of Kuwait. Therafter, succession became hereditary, ultimately confined to the Al Sabah lineage. The sheikh's authority was relatively diffuse. He was a leader but not a true ruler. He practised the system of *shura* and the town had a *majlis* in which the *ulama* (religious scholars) and the merchants played influential roles.

Kuwait flourished in the second half of the eighteenth century, becoming an important trading port. The economic growth was the result of several factors. First, the strategic position of Kuwait at the head of the Gulf and close to the Shatt al-Arab provided the Bani Utub and their associates with crucial opportunities to compete in the growing Eastern trade on both sea and land. Second, at that time the Bani Utub had a policy of free trade which encouraged neighbouring merchants to trade at the port of Kuwait. Finally, the Persians had occupied Basra in 1775, which had important implications for Kuwait's economy:

> The circumstances of the siege and occupation of Basra by the Persians had a far-reaching influence on Kuwait and Zubara [Zubair]. In the first place, direct relations were established between Kuwait and the British East India Company's representatives in the Gulf. Kuwait became important as a centre for nearly all the caravans carrying goods between Basra and Aleppo during the period 1775–1779. Because of the enmity existing between the British and the Persians, goods coming from India, which could have been sent to Abu Shahr for conveyance to Aleppo via

Basra, were unloaded at Zubara and Kuwait. This led to the accumulation of wealth at the two Utbi [*sic*] towns, and the jealousy of other sea-powers, especially the Bani Ka'b and the Arabs of Abu Shahr.[9]

The accumulation of capital enabled the emerging merchant class to finance and develop its boat-building industry. The merchants bought the raw material, teak plants, from India and financed the construction of vessels. At first, the nomadic and semi-nomadic tribes from nearby in Kuwait provided the necessary labour and supplied the merchants with goods suitable for export such as ghee and horses. Later, ship-builders arrived from Bahrain. They did not mix with the people of Kuwait but lived in a separate Shi'a community known as the *baharna*.[10]

Ship-building soon became one of the most profitable and respected industries. Towards the end of the eighteenth century, the number of vessels built and owned by Kuwaiti merchants matched that of any other newly established port in the Arabian Gulf. In 1841 it was reported that Kuwait had 31 large and 50 small vessels engaged in commerce and about 350 small vessels which were used for pearling and fishing.[11]

The availability of both capital and work attracted a large number of people from neighbouring countries, especially Bahrain, Iran and Iraq. Tribal groups from Central Arabia also came to settle in Kuwait, and slaves were brought from Africa. As a result, the population of Kuwait increased rapidly: in 1845 it was estimated at about 22,000 inhabitants.[12]

With the population increase, the economy diversified. It then became possible for the merchants, whose skills in trading brought them unexpected wealth, to finance the pearl-fishing industry. With sufficient labour and capital, a new group of merchants emerged: the *tawawish* (pearl merchants). They owned the vessels and financed each voyage, recruiting a captain, known as the *nukhoda*, usually from a well-established Sunni family. They also engaged a number of divers, haulers and cooks, for a season that lasted four to five months each summer.[13]

The financing of the pearl-fishing trips took two forms: the System of Fifths (Khamamis) and the System of Advances (Salafiya). The first operated on the basis of pre-fixed shares: after the pearls were sold, the ship-owner, usually the merchant, received one-fifth of the earnings; the captain and crew divided up the remainder on the basis of pre-arranged shares, allocating part to the diving tax instituted by the ruler, Sheikh Mubarak Al Sabah.[14]

The Salafiya relied on an advance cash payment that was meant to support the families of the divers and haulers during their absence. The payments took the form of *salaf* (loan payments). The *nukhoda* borrowed the money from the merchant, who charged excessive interest. If the catch of pearls was small and the *nukhoda* was unable to repay the loan, he was obliged to work for the same merchant again. Very often the *nukhoda* was unable to repay the merchant and a cycle of debt was begun: the divers and haulers were in debt to the captain, who in turn was in debt to the merchant. As long as the debts were not paid off, the divers and haulers were obliged to work for the same captain who in turn was obliged to sell the pearls to the same merchant. Accounts were kept of the loan payments and debts, and the debts were carried along a hereditary line. If, for instance, the diver died and the debt was not cleared, it passed on to his sons or brothers, who were then obliged to enter the pearling industry and work for the same *nukhoda* until the debt was paid off.[15]

This entire system benefited the merchants, who enjoyed a monopoly over the vessels and the marketing of pearls. Needless to say, the price paid for the pearls by the pearl merchants to the captains in the local market was far below the price these merchants realized in the main trading centres of Bahrain and Bombay.[16]

The *tujjar* (wholesale merchants), owners of large vessels, also benefited from the availability of cheap labour. They employed sailors and engaged a captain to supervise the commercial voyages which could sometimes last as long as seven to eight months. They loaded their vessels with dates from their own vast date plantations in Iraq and sold them in the ports of the lower Gulf and in East Africa. These merchants had enormous power over their crews and tolerated no protest.[17] Because they were dependent on the merchants for a living, the crew often felt obliged to agree to the merchants' conditions. As a result, the sailors were poor. In 1939 the British political agent in Kuwait reported, 'Some sailors are so poor that their youngsters have to sail with them as they cannot afford to keep them at home.'[18]

Social Organization

The internal structure of nomadic society—in terms both of residential unit and of kinship ties based on a common patrilineal descent—became firmly established in Kuwait. It was, however, the *ashira*, rather than the tribe as such, which evolved as the fundamental socio-economic unit.

Families lived close to each other, each in a distinct *farij* (neighbourhood). The town was divided into Hayy Sharq (People of the East), Hayy Qibli or Jibli (the West) and the Wasat (centre). The eastern part of the town was the domain of pearl merchants, *nukhoda*s and divers, while the western part was dominated by the wholesale merchants; the Al Sabah family lived in the central quarter.

The merchant families maintained strict endogamy, marrying only within their own lineage and with a preference for cross-cousin alliances. Only male members of the family could inherit family property, which was passed from father to son. They evolved as a distinct group and were recognized as such:

> Gradually the head of a *nakhoda*'s [*sic*] family may attain the status of a lesser merchant himself . . . but a *nakhoda* himself almost never becomes a merchant, a merchant's son never becomes a *nakhoda*.[19]

There were strict class rules. The merchants, wealthy and powerful, were the aristocrats of Kuwait. The ruling family was economically dependent upon them. In the late nineteenth century, British interference in the affairs of the sheikhdom disturbed the balance of power, giving rise to protest movements instigated by the merchants.

British Intervention and the Merchants' Uprising

Between 1899 and 1961 Britain played a crucial role in Kuwait's internal and external affairs. The historical circumstances which led to British intervention were decisive for the political development of the sheikhdom and of the entire Arabian Gulf region:

> Arabian shaykhs acquired additional power and prestige as a result of being recognized by the British as Trucial Shaykhs. Eventually, they adopted the title of *hakim* [ruler] and finally, at independence, the title of *amir*, combining the attributes of ruler, commander and prince.[20]

The first contact between Kuwait and Britain occurred in 1775. As pointed out earlier, during the Persian occupation of Basra, the representatives of the East India Company moved their trade to Kuwait for almost two years. Though the British authorities had a cordial relationship with the ruler of Kuwait, Sheikh Abdullah Al Sabah, the British had shown no immediate interest in strengthening their position in Kuwait. At that time, they were busy consolidating their control over the sea route to India and weakening the influence of their rival Western powers. For this reason, in 1789, Britain concluded a treaty with the Sultan of Muscat and Oman, the purpose of which was to exclude the French and the Dutch from the sultan's territory while they were at war with Britain.[21]

In 1800 a British agent of the East India Company was appointed on a permanent basis in Muscat. A series of treaties were later concluded between the British authorities and the principal rulers along the Arabian Gulf.[22] The most important was the peace treaty of 1820, which banned so-called acts of piracy and gave Britain the absolute right to punish such acts. While the treaty against piracy asserted British supremacy over the southern shore of the Gulf, it nevertheless left them vulnerable throughout the region. The Russian presence in Persia also presented a serious threat to the British Empire:

> Russia represented a danger to the British Empire on two accounts. First, because of Russia's complete control of northern Persia and its influence in Tehran, the British feared the possibility of the Russians extending that control to their own sphere of influence in southern Persia and the Persian Gulf. Second, Central Asia was watched with apprehension by the Indian government as the next most vulnerable area for a Russian military advance—an advance which might very well block the Indian gate to Asia.[23]

British fears of the Russian presence in the Gulf culminated in the 1899 Exclusive Agreement between the then ruler of Kuwait, Sheikh Mubarak, and the British authorities. Although Kuwait had been under the authority of the Ottoman Empire, both parties were anxious to conclude the treaty. For Mubarak, the agreement would keep the Turks at a safe distance and would consolidate his political power over Kuwait. For the British, it would ensure their full control over Central Arabia and would block Russian influence from spreading into the region. With the signing of the agreement, Mubarak bound himself, his heirs and his successors not to cede, sell, lease, mortgage or give away for occupation or any other purpose any portion of his territory to the government or subjects of any other power without the previous consent of the British government.

In 1904 Britain appointed a political agent to Kuwait; Ottoman protests cut short his stay and he left in May 1905. Later attempts proved more successful, and between 1909 and 1961 the British had several political agents in Kuwait. With the appointment of these officers, British policy moved beyond simply dealing with the external affairs of Kuwait.

Another important trend during this period was the merchants' development into an organized group seeking to re-establish their political authority. British involvement led to a weakening of the merchants' political power. Sheikh Mubarak rarely consulted them and continued to levy heavy taxes on imported goods and on all pearling vessels. The taxes led to general discontent among the *tawawish* and then to the migration, in 1910, of three leading pearl merchants, Hilal al-Mutayri, Shamlan bin Ali and Ibrahim bin Mudhif, along with their families and ship crews. Mubarak soon realized that if these wealthy pearl merchants failed to return, this would affect his own family who depended on the merchants for their livelihood in the form of tax revenues and customs duties on goods transported by sea. To convince them to return, Mubarak had to make many concessions. He even went in person to Bahrain to ask Hilal al-Mutayri, the wealthiest Kuwaiti pearl merchant, to return.[24]

Although he convinced the pearl merchants to return, Mubarak failed to institute any economic and political changes to appease the growing opposition to his regime. He continued to rule autocratically, and apart from inviting the American mission to open a medical service, made no further attempts to improve his administration of the town. Illiteracy was widespread and education was confined to the reading of the Quran. It was the merchants who, in 1912, took the initiative in establishing the first (private) school for boys, al-Mubarakiya. The school's curriculum included the Quran, local and Islamic traditions, canon law, ethics, Arabic reading, composition and grammar, arithmetic, geography, history and English.

The establishment of this school reflected the first conscious effort by the merchants to organize some education alongside the requirements of the economic sector. For almost 20 years al-Mubarakiya supplied the community with clerks, commercial correspondents and, at some stages, teachers. It failed, however, to spread literacy. The ruling family's unwillingness to support education made it difficult for the groups of pearl divers and sailors to send their children to school, since they had to rely on donations by the merchants for funding. Even after the foundation of the second school, al-Ahmadiya, in 1922, most children from poor families were left outside the world of literacy.

The merchants made a second attempt to restore political authority in 1921, following the sudden death of Sheikh Salim, the second son of Sheikh Mubarak. The merchants addressed a petition to the ruling family requesting the establishment of a Consultative Council (al-Majlis al-Istishari):

> The petition which was drafted after Salim's death was designed not only to re-establish consultation between the ruler and the notables, which existed prior to the era of Mubarak, but it was intended to institutionalize it. It is in this respect only that the step may be considered radical. Otherwise, the petition did not envision a broadening of the arena of politics. The hegemony of the ruling family and the merchant oligarchy remained intact.[25]

Sheikh Ahmad al-Jabir Al Sabah was nominated the new ruler of Kuwait; he immediately agreed to form a Consultative Council and 12 members were chosen from among the merchant community. The council, however, lasted only two months: the internal disputes and opposing views of members led to its disintegration and finally to its demise.

In spite of the failure to reach a consensus, the merchants maintained a strong cohesive network, which was important in the difficult years that lay ahead. The merchants began to experience economic difficulties in 1923, following the Saudi blockade; these grew worse in 1929 with the introduction of cultured pearls on the world market. The *tawawish* were so badly hit that they were unable to finance any education for their children. For almost five years, between 1931 and 1936, the schools were semi-closed for lack of funds.[26] In 1936 the merchants decided to make education the responsibility of an independent body. They unanimously agreed to raise their custom duties from 4.5 to 5 per cent, allotting the extra 0.5 per cent to education, and forming a Council for Education. For the first time, women were granted the right to education. In 1937 the first state school for girls was opened, with qualified Palestinian teachers being appointed. Following disagreements with Sheikh Ahmad, the Council for Education was dissolved.

This turn of events increased the tension between Sheikh Ahmad and the merchants, who, in 1938, formed an underground society called the National Bloc (al-Qutla al-Wataniya). The group drew much of its support from the Iraqi government, which at that time was anxious to gain control over Kuwait and to annex it as one of its territories. The National Bloc began to distribute leaflets printed in Iraq. In 1938 wall slogans in Kuwait began to call for reforms and the abdication of the ruler. One activist, al-Barrak, was arrested by the police and publicly flogged until he gave the names of three merchants with whom he was collaborating. Fearing reprisals, many merchants fled to Iraq. The National Bloc sent a petition to the ruler requesting immediate reforms and the establishment of a Legislative Council.

Fearing the end of his family's hegemony, Sheikh Ahmad turned to the British for help, but they pressured him to accept the demands of his people and to allow the formation of a Legislative Council. From the British point of view, the sooner the trouble was resolved, the fewer problems there would be for them and the ruling family. Furthermore, by pressing the sheikh to form a council, Britain hoped to kill two birds with one stone: to prevent a possible *coup d'état* and to win the sympathy of the opposition. On 18 July 1938 the British resident in the Gulf wrote:

> The movement against the sheikh was, as has been seen, overpowering, and a trial of strength between the popular party and the ruler, in which the former were certain to have won, was bound to have occurred, either now or in the near future. My advice to the shaikh to form a Council naturally fitted in with the plans of the popular party, and is indeed one of the main reasons that for the moment at all events they are extremely friendly towards us.[27]

The People's Legislative Council (Majlis al-Umma al-Tashri'i) was formed on 24 June 1938. Soon after its creation, it sent the ruler a document outlining its powers and responsibilities. This draft constitution was received with suspicion and fear by both the ruler and the British. After much hesitation, however, Sheikh Ahmad agreed to sign it.

Fearing a shift in the balance of power in favour of the council, the British authorities immediately sought to intervene in the power game. On 22 August 1938 the British resident in the Gulf wrote:

> The 'inaugural law' arms them [the council] with greater authority in respect of external affairs and dealings with foreigners than we can comfortably acknowledge . . . .[It is,] I suggest, essential to remove from the minds of the council any impression that we might regard them as the sole repository of authority in Kuwait, that we should prepare to deal with them to the exclusion of the shaikh, or that we should tolerate their interference with foreign affairs or their assumption of sole authority in respect of other matters.[28]

To maintain control and preserve its interests, Britain needed to reinforce the prestige and authority of the ruler at the expense of the People's Legislative Council. By instituting the sheikh as the 'constitutional head of state' and the 'sole repository of authority', the British destroyed the hope for any form of transition from autocrat to *primus inter pares* and laid down the configuration of political authority in Kuwait that continues to this day.

Nevertheless, the People's Legislative Council was declared to be the representative of the people of Kuwait. It held the power to ratify treaties, agreements and franchises, and introduced a series of reforms. Education was placed under the sponsorship of the government and a Department of Education was set up, to which all customs revenues were allotted. The diving tax was abolished. In addition, to stimulate competition and promote the development of local commerce, the council abolished all forms of monopolies.

Opposition to the council gradually grew, due partly to the secret encouragement of the British and Sheikh Ahmad. The opposition consisted mainly of wealthy wholesale merchants, members of the Shi'a community and the bedouin. In December 1938 an open confrontation between the council and the sheikh resulted in armed rebellion. Members of the council, who barricaded themselves in the fort, were forced to surrender. Some members were later arrested and imprisoned, while others took refuge in Iraq where they lived in exile until 1944.[29]

The council was dissolved to the great relief of both the British and the ruler of Saudi Arabia, King Abdul Aziz; he regarded the power of the council as 'ominous of encroaching, and uncontrolled, democracy in Arabia'.[30] This dissolution did not put an end to the *majlis* movement, however, nor did it diminish the scale of political protests. The 1950s were marked by heated protest movements which finally led to national independence and the establishment of a National Assembly in 1963. The discovery of oil and the growth of nationalism in the Arab world were major forces behind this turn of events. But although Kuwait was now an affluent society, its people remained as divided as they had been during the pre-oil era.

The 1950s represent an important phase in the history of Kuwait. This period saw the rise of voluntary associations and the reproduction of the pre-oil class divisions.

The Discovery of Oil and the Transformation of Kuwait (1950–1960)

Although oil was discovered at the Burgan field in 1938, it was not until the end of the Second World War that production started and Kuwait began its transformation under the reign of Sheikh Abdullah al-Salim Al Sabah (1950–65). His immediate policy was to create a welfare state which would provide free education, free medical services and housing grants for all citizens. He called in foreign experts and set up a large-scale development programme to modernize the country. Soon houses, schools, hospitals, power stations, government departments and many other public institutions were being built.

In their rush to modernize the city, foreign planners and architects demolished the old houses and put up Western-style buildings, ignoring such climatic factors as intense heat and sandstorms. The result was catastrophic: 'much Kuwaiti building in the Fifties was a precise reproduction of the kind of junk that was being run up in Europe, after the war'.[31] During this period, there was no supervision and no government control. The town was plunged into chaos. In 1954 the British political agent wrote:

> In a short space of time there has been imposed on this society an almost unimaginable increase of wealth, an influx of foreigners . . . , and finally the greatly increased impact of Arab nationalist ideas. These new elements have served to increase the power of the Shaikhs of the ruling family because they have access to the newly acquired wealth . . . .The rich merchants have become much richer and those less rich have become more envious. The poor have to compete with imported foreign labour

> . . . . Each department of the government is headed by a member of the ruling family. Practically no attempt has hitherto been made to restrict their expenditure either departmental or personal of the oil revenues. Moreover, in all matters they are above the law, and are accustomed to impose their personal authority by force if necessary.[32]

As a result of this abysmal lack of administration, the society simply continued the class divisions that had existed before the discovery of oil. In the early 1950s Sheikh Abdullah al-Salim set up the land purchase programme, intended to disseminate part of the oil revenues to the people of Kuwait. In anticipation of the government project, the merchants and members of the ruling family claimed large tracts of public land and registered them as private property in the newly created Department of Land Registry (al-Sijil al-Iqari). The lands were then sold to the government at highly inflated prices. Following the recommendations of the International Bank for Reconstruction and Development, Sheikh Abdullah decreased the funds allocated to the programme. The result was catastrophic. Many middle-income Kuwaitis, who had taken out loans to invest in land during the period of speculation, went bankrupt, thus losing their capacity to be entrepreneurs and becoming more dependent on the government.[33]

Using their handsome profits, the merchants formed new businesses and established commercial banks. By 1964 there were four privately owned banks. All their activities were organized on a kinship basis, with each group of families forming a business unit and monopolizing a particular trade.

For the majority of the Kuwaiti population, however, income from private business constituted only a small percentage of their total household income. The ex-*nukhoda*s, sailors and haulers formed the growing middle stratum of Kuwaiti society, comprising the categories of professionals and service workers: university lecturers, schoolteachers, administrators, social workers, and so on. However, not all who were unskilled labourers before the oil era succeeded in securing a modest income. Today 13 per cent of Kuwaiti households rely heavily on welfare assistance and the state still provides substantial aid:

> In addition to cash assistance, needy families may receive rent subsidies; reimbursement of loan and house finance instalments; subsidies for the purchase of clothes for their school-age children; subsidies for water and electricity consumption (79 per cent and 94 per cent of the actual costs, respectively); basic food necessities; and even oil subsidies for private car consumption.[34]

The development of the country led to the emergence of a new class: foreign workers. They did not intermarry with the Kuwaitis, but instead formed a class of their own, a class of skilled and unskilled labour which outnumbered the native Kuwaiti population. By 1965 Kuwaiti citizens made up only 47.1 per cent of the population, becoming a minority in their own country.

Another significant trend during this period of rapid change was the growth of voluntary associations. The most important were the Teachers Club (Nadi al-Mu'allimin), the National Cultural Club (Nadi al-Thaqafi al-Qaumi) and the Islamic Guidance Society (Jam'iyat al-Irshad al-Islamiya). All these organizations called for Arab unity, national independence and a constitutional government. The following extract, published in the early 1950s, summarizes the aim of the Kuwaiti nationalists:

> [O] all free people of our nation . . . ask for your rights. That is, we ask for the formation of a Constituent Assembly which will prepare a constitution and which will guarantee your natural freedom, put an end to the despotic rule and bring forth a national independent government which will be formed by the people themselves.[35]

Although they all called for national independence and constitutional government, each group represented a different line of nationalism. The young educated merchant-class men who founded the Teachers Club and issued two influential papers, *al-Ba'tha* (The Mission; 1946) and *al-Ra'id* (The Pioneers; 1952), adhered to a more liberal national ideology, reminiscent of that of the Arab national bourgeoisie. These young men, who had been educated in Egypt, did not call for radical political changes; they simply wanted a constitutional government and a more controlled national economy. As we shall see in Chapter 2, they also pressed for the emancipation of Kuwaiti women.

The National Cultural Club was less homogeneous and more radical. It was composed of Arab expatriates and educated young Kuwaiti men recruited from the emerging middle stratum. Their nationalism was coloured with socialist ideals: they wanted the government to give equal rights to Arab expatriates, and called for a fair distribution of the national wealth. For instance, in an article published in their magazine *Sada al-Iman* (The Echo of Faith) in September 1954, the club leaders stated:

> We appeal to the government to turn toward these miserable nationals and do something—anything—for their sake. It is not fair to waste the wealth in things that we do not need at a time when our compatriots do not have

> proper lodgings. In these huts, shacks and ruins, there are children of both sexes who cannot go to school because they live far, far indeed from schools. Most of them are living outside the city wall.[36]

The third organization, which was to play an influential role from the mid-1970s onwards, was the Social Reform Society. It was founded by a wealthy merchant, Abdul Aziz al-Mutawa‘, who established strong ties with the Ikhwan, the Muslim Brotherhood movement of Egypt. In 1956, when the Ikhwan organization in Egypt came under attack, many of its members settled temporarily in Kuwait and made the Islamic Guidance Society their headquarters. The watchwords of the society were Islam and Arab nationalism. Arabism and Islam were not conceived as opposed to each other; Arab unity was seen as a prelude to Islamic unity. The society urged the leading states of the Middle East, including Kuwait, to co-operate to further the cause of Islam which, they argued, had been weakened by 'imperialism'.

In 1956 these organizations held the first political demonstration to protest at Britain's involvement in the Suez crisis. The government ordered the police to disperse the crowd and arrest the demonstrators, but this police intervention provoked general indignation. The head of the police force, himself an ardent advocate of Arab nationalism, resigned. Explosives were set off in Ahmadi near the oil refineries, causing severe damage, and the government deported many Arab expatriates.

Despite government threats of further political reprisals, Kuwaiti nationalists and Arab expatriates held a rally in 1959 at the Shuwaikh secondary school to commemorate the first anniversary of the creation of the United Arab Republic. In lengthy political speeches, they called for Arab unity and attacked the autocratic regime of the ruling family. The sheikh took a much harder line this time. Voluntary associations and the press were banned and the elections to the administrative councils were cancelled.

National Independence

On 19 June 1961, amid widespread Arab nationalist sentiment and internal political agitation, Sheikh Abdullah al-Salim signed a Treaty of Independence with Britain, abrogating the 1899 Exclusive Agreement. The signing of the treaty was followed by sweeping reforms to appease the growing opposition to the regime and to maintain order: the People's Legislative Council was restored and the voluntary associations were institutionalized.

The Merchants and the Constitutional Government

Sheikh Abdullah al-Salim formed a provisional Constituent Assembly to draft the state constitution, which was approved on 11 November 1962. The constitution designated Kuwait as a hereditary emirate and confined succession to the descendants of the late Mubarak Al Sabah. The amir was declared head of state and supreme commander of the armed forces. The heir apparent was to be nominated by the amir within one year of his accession, and approved by a simple majority of the National Assembly.

The constitution defined three powers: executive, legislative and judicial. Executive powers were confined to the amir, the Council of Ministers which was appointed by the amir, and the prime minister (by tradition, always the crown prince). Legislative powers were vested in the amir and the National Assembly, which was to be elected every four years. But the amir had the power to adjourn the National Assembly for not more than one month, or to dissolve it by decree. The first general elections were held on 23 January 1963: only Kuwaiti men were eligible to vote or stand for election.

The constitution guaranteed the right to education and employment (provided by the state) for all Kuwaiti citizens, both men and women. It further guaranteed personal liberty, freedom of religion, and freedom of the press and association, but forbade political parties. The Citizenship Law, introduced in 1959, restricted Kuwaiti nationality to people who had lived in Kuwait before 1920 and had resided there until 1959.

The constitution and national independence brought a new dimension to the relationship between the merchant class and the ruling family: that of political alliances: 'the Council of Ministers provided the mechanism for bringing into direct government participation and post-oil economic organization members of the pre-oil dominant class'.[37] To this day, the merchant class remains the most powerful economic stratum, controlling the country's major trading companies and financial institutions.

The Institutionalization of Voluntary Associations

After independence in 1961, the government allowed voluntary associations to operate. The Islamic Guidance Society re-emerged under the name of Social Reform Society (Jam'iyat al-Islah al-Ijtima'i) and the National Cultural Club was renamed the Independence Club (Nadi al-Istiqlal). But this time, voluntary associations were put under direct government supervision.

The depoliticization of voluntary associations had been one of the government's main concerns. The events of the 1950s showed that these organizations could be used as a base for political struggle and highlighted the potential political power of Arab expatriates. For this reason, in 1962, a new law was introduced to curtail the power of voluntary associations and to remove Arab expatriates from positions of authority.

The 1962 law—partially amended in 1965 and still in force at the time of writing—confines the activities of voluntary associations to 'social welfare purposes'. Article 1 defines voluntary associations as organized societies and clubs that continue for a definite or indefinite period, consist of natural and corporate persons, for an object other than obtaining a material profit, and aim at carrying out social, cultural, religious or sports activities.

Voluntary associations are strictly forbidden from indulging in any kind of political or religious activity that could endanger the stability of the state. Every voluntary organization must have a constitution to which its members strictly adhere and a board of directors elected every four years (or less) by a general assembly. The board of directors must consist of a president, a vice-president, a treasurer and other equally important officials. The right to hold office is confined to Kuwaiti nationals. Non-Kuwaiti nationals cannot take part in general assemblies, so they cannot vote or stand for office.

Those who wish to establish an association must be Kuwaiti nationals, over 18 years of age, and must submit their names and addresses, along with the group's constitution, to the Ministry of Social Affairs and Labour. The ministry has full control and power over the emerging associations. It has the power to refuse to license an association, or to terminate an association if it is found not to be beneficial to the society as a whole or not to be abiding by its constitution. On the other hand, the ministry is bound to provide premises and funds to support the associations in their endeavours. As of 1987, 53 voluntary associations had registered, including professional associations, welfare and charitable associations, educational societies, recreational and hobbies societies, religious (Islamic) societies, women's societies and music and drama societies.[38]

On average, an association receives an annual grant of KD12,000.[39] There are a few exceptions: the Science Club, the Red Crescent Society, the Society for the Handicapped and the Teachers Society receive much higher government funding, because they are considered essential and beneficial both to their members and to the society at large. In 1989 the Science Club received an annual grant of KD180,000. The Red Crescent Society, the Teachers Society and the Society for the Handicapped each received KD100,000.

In 1988 the total membership of 52 voluntary associations numbered 25,033,[40] with men making up the majority (66 per cent) of the total membership. The total membership of women's organizations was relatively low, numbering 1,752. In 1985 the Kuwaiti female population between the ages of 18 and 50 was estimated to be 179,582.[41] Thus only 3 per cent of the female population were involved in women's organizations.

Women tend to be predominant in professional and educational associations, and in certain welfare associations, such as the Society for the Handicapped and the Centre for Child Evaluation and Teaching. Charitable organizations are mostly religious and therefore tend to exclude women from direct participation. As an official of a charitable organization explained, 'Women are our main fund-raisers but we do not consider them for membership.' All the leadership positions of the religious organizations are strictly confined to men. With the exception of the women's organizations and the Nurses Society, which are chiefly composed of women, none of the existing voluntary associations has ever had a female president. In 1988, 93 per cent of all the board members were men and a mere 7 per cent were women.

The low level of female involvement in committees is equally noticeable. In 1988, 77 per cent of all active committee members were men and only 23 per cent were women. Furthermore, women are very rarely in positions of authority: 84 per cent of all the committees were headed by men. It is only in the social welfare organizations, mentioned above, that women tend to have much wider opportunities for holding office, simply because they outnumber male members.

Most of the voluntary organizations pursue some kind of exclusionary tactics aimed at either removing women from influential positions or preventing a particular group from gaining control. As will be discussed in more detail in Chapter 4, even the women's organizations have exclusive policies on membership, which explains the relatively low level of female participation. Exclusionary tactics form part of the strategy of control. For instance, to maintain male control over an association, male leaders seek to exclude women from direct participation; this, in turn, has the effect of reducing women's desire to join the voluntary associations. The exclusion of women is based on the male belief that women are not capable of handling political or administrative reponsibilities and that they are better suited to social welfare activities, fund-raising or working with other women. Such beliefs are linked to the male desire to exclude women from political participation and from the organizations under their control.

Voluntary organizations have remained an essential component of the political arena. The control of these associations is linked to political control and the exercise of political power. As will be shown below, in spite of increasing state control, the voluntary organizations have continued to assume a political role. Throughout the 1960s and 1970s Kuwaiti nationalists used the network of voluntary associations to win popular support and to express opposition to the regime. Indeed, these associations helped to widen and strengthen the nationalist movement. In the mid-1970s the government decision to close these associations and dissolve the National Assembly came as a real blow to the nationalists and has significantly weakened their movement.

The State, Voluntary Associations and Political Conflict

With the reinforcement of state control, the voluntary associations did not become mere extensions of state authority. That is, they did not cease to be a threat to the state; on the contrary, they continued to operate as secondary powers. It is because political parties are prohibited and the voluntary associations remain the only legitimate means of public activity that they play such an important role in the political arena. The struggle between the Kuwaiti nationalists and the Ikhwan for control of the voluntary associations, and the way the government has responded to their threats, provide an interesting illustration of the role of these associations as secondary powers.

Between 1963 and 1976 the young Kuwaiti nationalists formed many associations. In addition to the Independence Club, they established, to name just a few, the National Union of Kuwaiti Students, the Graduates Society, the Teachers Society, the Lawyers Society and the General Union of Kuwaiti Workers. These were more than social clubs. They offered a public forum in which to express opposition to the regime, to lobby for political support and to raise public consciousness on national and regional issues:

> Considerable activity that is political in nature takes place within these organizations. Much of this activity consists of little more than gossiping about the political issues of the day, but significant are disguised campaigning for political candidates, lobbying for legislation and administrative proposals, and even clandestine organizing of demonstrations.[42]

Throughout the 1960s and mid-1970s the nationalists played the role of the opposition both inside and outside the National Assembly. They had many demands: political unity with the other Arab states, nationalization of the oil industry, better job opportunities, the enfranchisement of women, the right to form unions and political parties, freedom of the press and more rights for Arab expatriates. The opposition posed a significant political challenge to the government.

By the mid-1970s, the situation had become intolerable for the government. In the National Assembly, the nationalists had won new allies and opposed the government on many issues. The students became increasingly politicized and militant, regularly protesting in solidarity with the Palestinians and with regional opposition groups in Bahrain, Oman and the rest of the Gulf.[43] There were signs of political instability throughout the Middle East, as a civil war erupted in Lebanon and Syria intervened. Arab unity was quickly becoming a thing of the past.

Faced with persistent attacks both inside and outside the National Assembly and with political instability in the Arab world, the government responded with draconian measures. In August 1976 the Assembly was dissolved, several articles of the constitution were suspended and freedom of the press was curtailed. The nationalists objected to the dissolution of the Assembly and issued statements of protest. The government responded with more repressive measures:

> In September the Trade Union Federation president was arrested with other union members for leafleting against press curbs and the dissolution. In October the government replaced the Teachers Society board and closed the student union paper. In November it dissolved the boards of the writers, lawyers and journalists associations, and suspended the editors of *al-Watan* and *al-Tali'a*. In July the ANM Istiqlal Club was dissolved.[44]

In its attempts to suppress Arab nationalism, the government encouraged the proliferation of Islamic beliefs:

> The regime had perceived the vocal nationalist opposition group in the National Assemblies of the 1960s and 1970s as a particularly potent and worrisome threat. Government strategy in restoring the assembly seemed directed at preventing the nationalists from regaining a platform for anti-government rhetoric, even to the point of permitting more freedom for the Islamics as a counterweight.[45]

The Jam'iyat al-Islah, which represents the Muslim Brotherhood movement (Ikhwan), was still allowed to operate. Between 1976 and 1980, in the absence of political opposition, the *imams* (mosque preachers) gained power and influence within the community, and their Friday *khutba* (sermon) became very popular. The Islah increased its membership. The power of the Ikhwan was particularly felt in the university where, in 1979, they succeeded in defeating the nationalist groups in the election for the Student Union.

Ironically, after having reduced the threat of the Kuwaiti nationalists, the government found itself confronted by a new political challenge, this time from the Islamic movement. At a time when the Islamic revolution was taking place in neighbouring Iran, the strength of the Ikhwan must have caused the government some concern as it responded to the Islamic challenge 'by taking a more Islamist posture itself, tightening the ban on alcohol, increasing religious broadcasting, and supporting the Kuwait Finance House, Kuwait's first Islamic bank'.[46]

In 1981 a group known as the Salaf formed the Islamic Heritage Society (Jam'iyat al-Turath al-Islamiya). The Salafiya movement is equivalent to the late nineteenth-century Wahhabi movement, and seeks a return to the roots of Islam as laid down in the *hadith* (sayings of the Prophet) and codified in the Shari'a. The Salaf are more conservative and traditionalist than the Ikhwan, the latter presenting a more politicized aspect of Islam that aims to bring about changes at both the social and political levels.

Throughout the 1980s the government seemed particularly anxious to control the Islamic groups. In the 1985 election to the restored National Assembly, the government showed its concern by giving its full support to the one group capable of deflecting the religious movement: the progressives.[47] This time, the religious groups did not do well in the elections and several of their candidates were defeated. The nationalists made a small but significant appearance in the National Assembly. Nevertheless, the government once again put an end to the people's rights to political participation. On 3 July 1986 the Amir of Kuwait, Sheikh Jabir al-Ahmad al-Jabir Al Sabah, suspended the National Assembly and severely curtailed freedom of the press.

Conclusion

The rise of the oil economy did not alter the social stratification of the traditional Kuwaiti community. On the contrary, it deepened the social divisions and brought new elements into its core: while the lifestyle of Kuwaiti nationals has improved dramatically, the unequal distribution of wealth, privileges and power has remained. Wealth and power continue to be concentrated in the hands of the ruling family and the merchant class.

It was in the context of the struggle for political power that the voluntary associations first emerged. They were established by the merchant class as a forum in which to voice their grievances and to mount opposition to the regime. During the economic transformation of the early 1950s, the voluntary associations were again used by the merchant class to initiate and press for political change. They were later appropriated by the nationalists and the Muslim revivalists, who represented the new political forces. In spite of government control, the associations remain an important vehicle of social change and the loci of political struggles.

2
The Lives and Experiences of Kuwaiti Women

In Kuwait, the world of women has been so cut off from that of men that any history of Kuwait requires a separate chapter devoted to women. Women lived their lives from birth to death in the mud-walled town. They knew nothing of the seafaring voyages, of the charm of Indian cities or the port of Zanzibar, except perhaps what they heard from their male relatives. The town was part of women's lives—not of all women but of those who needed to earn a living; wealthy women lived secluded in their own courtyards. When in the mid-1950s the old houses were being demolished to make room for modern buildings, a young merchant-class woman exclaimed, much to the bewilderment of an English resident, 'Let them be demolished! Who wants them now? It is the new Kuwait and not the old which is worthy of admiration!'[1] The old town represented everything that Kuwaiti women wanted to forget—it symbolized their seclusion and reminded them of their oppression.

The Life of Women during the Pre-oil Era

The town of Kuwait had an unusual character. It was built of mud, divided into quarters and surrounded by a thick wall to prevent bedouin raids. In each quarter lived groups of families related by ties of kinship and/or marriage. The merchants and the ruling family lived in large houses facing the sea front. The *nukhoda*s, sailors and labourers lived in smaller houses.

From the outside, all the houses looked very similar, uninviting and secretive. They were the colour of the earth and had 'only one ground floor, but appear[ed] higher owing to a parapet-wall enclosing the roof'.[2] They were turned inwards, facing a courtyard. Large houses had two courtyards, one reserved for men and the other for women. The only part of the house which might have windows was the men's *diwaniya* (reception room).

Mechanisms of Social Control

The women of wealthy families lived in their own courtyards, secluded from the outside world and confined to a section of the house where there were no windows so that their voices could not be heard. The Kuwaiti historian Yusuf al-Qinaie reported that it was considered *aib* (shameful) to let women's voices be heard. Women should not be seen or even heard by men who were not their relatives.[3] They were also strictly forbidden to leave their courtyards, except occasionally to visit their relatives 'and perhaps once a year in the spring to go picnicking in the desert'.[4]

The strict seclusion was a way of controlling women. The trading voyages took men away for long periods of time, leaving women and children behind. Hence it was important for the merchant families that their women be safely protected, hidden and unheard of during the men's prolonged absence. Thus the houses were built to give women maximum protection, to conceal their existence and give them enough room to move around.

To prevent their women from having to venture outside the household, the merchants placed at their disposal a number of servants and slaves to do the daily shopping, including all the domestic work. As a result, wealthy women had little to do, apart from supervising the servants; there in their own courtyards, idle and secluded, they lived with their grandmothers, mothers, sisters and sisters-in-law and the children. In each household, a number of families lived together. A son would rarely leave his parental home; he would bring his wife to live with his family.

But seclusion was only one form of social control. Women from more modest households were not entirely secluded, for most of these households could not afford servants. This meant that women had to do all the domestic work, such as cooking and cleaning the courtyard. They also had to go to the *suq* (market) to buy the daily supply of food, fetch the drinking water from the supply boats and take the family's clothes to the beach to wash them. They often did the work in groups and by rotation to break the monotony.[5]

Whenever they needed to go out to make their visits or go to town, women had to drape themselves in a long black cloak, known as the *abbaya*, and veil their faces with a thick black cloth, the *boshiya*. The veil provided another form of protection which men considered essential if their women were to be respected and respectable. A woman from a respectable family was not supposed to uncover her face to an unrelated man. If she dared to do so, she could face painful punishment, since being unveiled was considered an act of dishonour. A man had the right to punish any woman who brought his family name into disrepute. Ina Robertson, who lived in Kuwait in the 1930s, wrote about a young woman named Dana who was killed by her own husband for having allegedly allowed herself to be seen by an unrelated man:

> Dana was married to a husband who had borrowed money. The creditor finally decided to humiliate him by saying that he had seen his wife's face that morning. On hearing this, the husband turned quickly on his heel, his heart aflame with anger against the wife who would so dishonor his name. Dana, who was cooking over the charcoal brazier, smiled as he approached. The smile was scarcely frozen into terror before a club came down on her head and killed her.[6]

Similarly, the slightest rumour that a woman had committed a moral offence could endanger her life, but no legal action would be taken against the man. According to Zahra Freeth, 'it has always been the privilege of the male head of the family to wipe out a female member who sullies the family honour'.[7] Robertson describes how a young man named Abdul Wahab was responsible for his sister's death after overhearing his friend Nasr propose a clandestine meeting:

> Abdul Wahab was fond of his sister from childhood, and often discussed problems with her in later years. On one occasion he heard Nasr state that the earth was round and revolved around the sun. He was most interested in this theory, and went to get an orange so that Nasr might demonstrate the principle. When Abdul Wahab returned he overheard Nasr tell his sister to meet him at a secret place that evening. Abdul Wahab reported this incident to his eldest brother, and suggested that the girl be married to Nasr without delay. In the morning, however, the girl was shot by her eldest brother with no further comment.[8]

The death threat acted as a powerful mechanism of social control. For centuries, it has kept women 'in their place' and reinforced their subordination to men.

The Devaluation of Women

Not only were women controlled; they were also devalued. They played no role in the seafaring economy and lived on the periphery of the male community. According to al-Qinaie, 'men viewed them as useless chattels'.[9] The devaluation of women was evident at the birth of a child. If it was a boy, the men celebrated; for days, male relatives and friends would call upon the 'lucky' father in his *diwaniya* to congratulate him. The birth of a daughter, however, caused no celebration. On the contrary:

> A woman who bore only girls faced the threat of either a divorce or the possibility of her husband having another wife. Consensus not only allowed but commanded such an action on the part of a man.[10]

A boy was soon integrated into the male seafaring community where he would begin his apprenticeship at the age of 10 under his father's supervision. On the other hand, as soon as a girl reached puberty, she was forbidden to play in the streets with the boys and had to retire with the other females to the secluded courtyard. If she happened to be the eldest daughter, she was immediately married to a male cousin. As in the desert, cross-cousin marriage was the norm and no one dared challenge it: 'a young girl was forced into marriage, independently of her wishes, particularly to her first paternal cousin even if he was ugly in demeanour and immoral in behaviour'.[11] But if she was not the eldest and there was no suitable bridegroom in sight, the parents would have to call upon the services of a *khataba* (marriage broker). The *khataba*, usually an old woman, would pay visits to various families and report to the interested family about prospective bridegrooms.

The merchant community had little need for the *khataba*; they preferred to marry among themselves and often had a clear idea of who was to be married to whom. As noted in the previous chapter, however rich the son of a *nukhoda* might be, he could never marry the daughter of a merchant. It was important for the merchant community to marry only among themselves, or even within their own lineage, if they were to maintain their privileges and preserve their 'racial purity' (i.e. being *asil*), which set them apart from others and perpetuated their power.

The young girl was kept in the dark about her coming marriage and had no say in the affair. It was the senior male members of her extended family who would make the arrangements for the wedding, assess the suitability of the bridegroom, gather information about his family *asl* and set the price of the *mahr* (dowry). The wedding usually took place on a Friday or a Monday. It was customary for bride and bridegroom not to have seen each other previously or have the faintest idea of what the other looked like. According to al-Qinaie, 'Conjugal happiness was a matter of chance and fate, with one happy marriage to a thousand, because neither the man nor the woman would have seen each other prior to the wedding night.'[12]

On the day of the wedding, the bride's mother and other female relatives spent the morning preparing the bride. For hours, the young woman was bathed and perfumed. Her hands and feet were coloured with geometrical henna designs, her eyes darkened with kohl, her lips reddened and her hair carefully plaited.[13] She was then dressed and covered with jewellery, from gold headband to gold bracelets on her wrists and ankles. Those who could not afford wedding jewellery could always borrow them from a rich woman, the wife of a sheikh or a merchant.

In the evening the bridegroom would make his way to the bride's house, followed in procession by his male relatives and a group of drummers, 'singing and clapping their hands in rhythm with the drums'.[14] There they feasted and later the bridegroom, cheered on by loud singing and clapping, was pushed into the bride's bedroom.

Starting the next day and continuing for five to six days, the young bride would receive friends and relatives, dressed in her best silk clothes and finest jewellery, before she was taken to her *hamula* (husband's family). There she would stay for the rest of her life with her mother- and sisters-in-law. Her duty was now to serve her new family. She was allowed to visit her own family only once a week, with her husband as escort. The couple would usually leave at dawn and return in the evening so that no one could catch a glimpse of the married woman, no matter how heavily veiled she might be.[15]

Forced into marriage at a very young age with a modest *mahr* that she was allowed to keep, a woman could expect very little from her paternal family. She was stripped of her right to inheritance despite the Islamic law which entitles women to a share of an inheritance half that of the man's. A father would only leave his property to his sons, and 'if he left funds for charity, his sons would be the guardians of the trust and not his daughters even if the latter were more virtuous and more trustworthy'.[16]

A Community Apart

Drawn together in an arid town where the sea provided the main source of livelihood from which they were excluded, women created a community of their own, tied together by a chain of asymmetrical dependency relationships. Women from poor households depended upon rich women to earn a living, however meagre, and wealthy households depended on the services of the poor. There was so much poverty and so few opportunities for work that poor women 'either worked as servants in wealthy households or begged'.[17] It was common to see women wandering the streets, begging for food or charity.

In spite of the limited opportunities, women from modest and poor households nevertheless attempted to develop certain skills. They worked, though in relatively small numbers, as midwives, *khatabas* and dressmakers. Others were involved in petty trading as pedlars or market traders. At the Suq Wajef, also known as Suq al-Harim (the women's market), female traders gathered to sell their goods: silk fabrics, kohl, henna, wooden combs and many other items brought by their husbands from their trading voyages. A pedlar would sometimes work as a link between the female traders of the Suq Wajef and the dressmakers. The pedlar would agree with a female trader to have a certain quantity of cloth made up, either as long dresses or as *dishdashas* (men's traditional garment). The pedlar would then take the textiles to the dressmaker. Some time later, the pedlar would collect the items, pay the dressmaker and then give the clothes to the trader, in return for a commission amounting to 10 per cent of the total price.[18]

Petty trading did not remain the main source of livelihood for women. In 1916 Amina al-Omar, who had been taught the Quran by her father, decided to teach girls how to recite the Quran as a way to earn a living. There were already many Quranic boys' schools but none for girls. The first Quranic boys' school was established as early as 1887 but the male community had made no attempt to give women similar educational opportunities.

Al-Omar's attempt was so successful that many women from modest houses began to work as *mutawa'as* (religious instructors) and to use their households as schools. Very soon, in every quarter, there was a *mutawa'a* who taught from her home, marking the beginning of the teaching profession for women.[19] The *mutawa'a,* who usually had about 10 to 20 students, received a fee of between 2 and 5 rupees per pupil, depending on each girl's family income.

Women's education took another step forward when in 1926 Mrs Aisha al-Ismiri, the wife of a Turkish headmaster, decided to open a school for girls. She spoke to the amir, who agreed to provide her with small premises in the al-Mubarakiya quarter. Mrs al-Ismiri taught reading and writing, and gave lessons in embroidery and dressmaking. According to Huda Nashif, 'the school was very successful and attracted a great number of girls to the extent that some girls were turned down due to shortage of accommodation'.[20] A few years later, one of al-Ismiri's students called Badria al-Attiqi, who was only 14 years old but had successfully completed her studies, opened her own school in her house. Soon many other women set up their own private schools to teach other girls what they had learned.

Among the most famous schools was that of Mariam al-Askar, who used printed books for the first time in Kuwait.

Teaching provided women with a badly needed income, given their economic situation. At the same time, it gave young girls access to an education which the authorities and the male community considered to be useful but not as important as that of boys. It was not until 1937 that the first state school for girls was set up at the initiative of the Council for Education. For nearly six months, however, the primary school had no pupils and the Palestinian teachers were idle. The men of the community had little interest in giving women more than a basic religious education. Had it not been for the discovery of oil, which led to a restructuring of the whole community, women's education would undoubtedly have remained confined to a relatively simple level.

The Practice of Zar *and the Search for an Alternative Source of Power*

There is historical evidence that women believed in witches and in *jinn* (demons) and practised the *zar* (spiritual possession). They believed that witches could fly in the night and many went so far as to claim that they had seen a witch flying. They also believed that *jinn* hide in the night, waiting at every street corner, sometimes taking the form of sheep. Robertson reported that 'a woman hurrying home after nightfall is terrified if she sees a sheep following her, thinking that a jiini has incorporated itself into that body'.[21]

The *zar* is a spirit which, it was believed, could possess people, particularly women, and could speak a language that only the *sheikha* (spiritual healer) could understand:

> If a woman fell ill, it was attributed to the *zar* and it was the *sheikha* of the *zar* who was at the service of the patient; she massaged her body with oil and organized a party where women, who themselves were possessed by the *zar*, danced and played the tambourine.[22]

The dancing ceremony organized by the *sheikha* was part of a ritual to tame the spirit and to cure the person who had succumbed to his power. To cure simply meant to put the spirit under control, i.e. to 'respond to his demands'. The spirits, it was said, are malicious. They want all sorts of things such as expensive jewellery or silk garments, and it is only when they get what they want that the person is cured. Possessed women, who put the spirit under control, had their own gatherings during which they feasted and danced to the rhythm of tambourines.

It was also believed that the spirit had the power to cure a sick person. Al-Qinaie provides another example of how women practised the *zar*. A woman he knew had tuberculosis:

> The *sheikha* had asked her to organize a *zar* ceremony; and if the *zar* possessed her, the *sheikha* would then persuade the *zar* to cure her by trying to please him and give him whatever he wished until the woman was cured. Several ceremonies were organized but the *zar* did not descend upon her. At the last ceremony, the sick woman began to move her head and dance while seated. The women of the party burst into tears of joy. The *sheikha* moved closer to the sick woman to try to please the *zar* and to see to his demands. The sick woman quickly said that it was not that she had the *zar* but just that she felt her spirits lifted and wanted to dance. The women of the party went to spread the news that the *zar* had possessed her and spoken through her. The sick woman was not cured and later died.[23]

According to al-Qinaie, the reason that so many women believed in such superstitions was that the *zar* ceremony had cured some of them.

Far from being mere superstition, the practice of *zar* involves the manipulation of power relations in favour of the powerless. In other words, 'spirit possession is a form of bargaining from a position of weakness.'[24] In her account of Kuwaiti women during the 1930s, Robertson reports:

> Some women are astute enough to profit by the belief in demons. They tell their husbands or friends that the devil which possesses them wants a silk garment (*thob*), or a sheep or something of the kind, and because of the superstitious fear of such spirits, the women generally receive whatever they demand.[25]

Hence, through the intermediary of spirits, women were able to make demands on men which might otherwise be denied. More importantly, in doing so, they put the blame on the spirits and not on themselves, therefore escaping any form of punishment or refusal and, at the same time, achieving their aims. Thus they became 'totally blameless; responsibility lies not in them, but with the spirits'.[26] Such an astute practice gave women the chance to exercise their malice and manipulate men without running the risk of being punished.

But women did not simply attempt to make indirect demands on men; they went so far as to claim supernatural powers. Old Kuwait was filled with tales of witches, and women found pleasure in spreading such stories, however fictitious they might be, as if to validate their own power and make men fear them. It worked: the more women made up stories about each others' supernatural powers, the more men were inclined to believe them. Among the most famous stories was that of a woman whom everyone believed was a witch:

> She had a brother who followed her wherever she went. He was vicious and she did not like him, so she turned him into a sheep and tied him up in the courtyard. The vicious brother disappeared but everyone knew of her doings. The eldest brother intervened and told her if she did not bring her brother back to his human form he would kill her. The witch returned him.[27]

Whether or not the witch brought her brother back out of fear is not the issue. The idea that the story was meant to spread was that a woman could ruin a man's life if he made her unhappy and that women have as much power as men to destroy someone. Men did indeed fear such power.

In the absence of institutionalized means to express their anger and protest at men's control, the practice of *zar* and sorcery has offered an alternative means for women to seek revenge and gain power. These practices are widespread in those societies where women have little power and are generally excluded from the men's world.[28] The fact that Kuwaiti men tolerated such malicious practices on the part of women was partly because they themselves believed in *jinn*. The Quran refers to *jinn* and, according to al-Qinaie, many men believed in their existence.

Al-Nahda *and the Call for the Emancipation of Women (1950–1960)*

In the years following the discovery of oil, the lives of women gradually changed. Those who initiated such changes and radically transformed the lives of women were the newly educated Kuwaiti men, all of whom came from well-established merchant families. They had read the works of Qasim Amin, Georges Hanna, Taha Hussein and many other Arab intellectuals, and were deeply influenced by their idea of *nahda* (progress) and women's emancipation.

In 1946, while studying in Cairo, they founded a weekly paper and called it *al-Ba'tha* (The Mission). A few years later, on their return to Kuwait, they established the Teachers Club and in 1952 published *al-Ra'id* (The Pioneers), a weekly magazine. This move was soon followed by other newly educated young men who launched *al-Iman* (Faith) in 1953, *al-Fajr* (Dawn) in 1955 and *al-Sha'b* (The People) in 1957.[29] This was a period of growing Arab nationalism. Everywhere in the Arab world, struggles for national independence were emerging.

As noted earlier, the kind of nationalism that these men of the merchant class espoused replicated that of other nationalistic bourgeois Arabs of the *nahda* period. Like Qasim Amin and many other Westernized Arab intellectuals, they set themselves the task of lifting their societies from what they saw as a state of *rajiya* (backwardness) to a state of *nahda* (progress) and civilization.

In an editorial in March 1950 Abdul Aziz Hussein, the editor of *al-Ba'tha,* wrote:

> In this country, two social groups have been formed: one is an aware group of young men who are sufficiently well-educated; the other is the older generation whose lives have been shaped by experience. It is upon these two groups that the country depends as a directional popular force, as an instrument which will bring the notion of a new life closer to people's minds. But if harmony and homogeneity are to be realized in our expected *nahda*, both groups need to work together. . . . Aren't we right to yearn for an ideal *nahda* which will elevate the standard of the country to that of civilized nations?[30]

The whole idea of *nahda* was to move forward, to break away from old traditions and customs, and to build a modern infrastructure, or more precisely, to adopt a Western model of civilization. The concepts used to describe the world and justify the necessity for change were *taqaddum* (progress) versus *rajiya* (backwardness). The latter was interpreted as being the result of rigid traditions and ignorance, whereas *taqaddum* was equated with scientific knowledge, cultural advancement and democracy. The aim was to modernize Kuwaiti society and end its isolation from the civilized world.[31]

Central to the realization of *nahda* was the emancipation of women. There could be no *nahda* without women's emancipation, just as there could be no progress without dismantling existing traditions and customs. These two processes were regarded as firmly interrelated. The emancipation of women was part of a struggle in which they were engaged, defined as being 'between knowledge and ignorance, between progress and backwardness, between modern lifestyles and retrograde traditions and customs'.[32]

The arguments advanced to justify women's emancipation were similar to those of Western advocates of women's rights in the late nineteenth and early twentieth centuries. They centred round two poles which have been described as 'the sameness and difference arguments'.[33] 'Sameness' refers to the sense that men and women are considered to be almost identical:

> Like a man, a woman also has a brain and feelings. They are both similar in their characters, their thinking and feelings and there is no need to differentiate between them; and if there is any reason to do so, this is mainly due to man's love for domination and power and it is not based upon logic and religion.[34]

Women, it was claimed, were endowed with the same abilities as men, being neither less intelligent nor less strong. Nothing, it was argued, proves that women are inferior to men:

> Look at the societies which are ahead of us in progress and civilization; you will see that both sexes are working together to achieve their societies' objectives. . . . There is no one who says that a woman has less intelligence than men, or has a weaker constitution. On the contrary, it has been proved that she is not at all less intelligent or less strong than men. The precision and wisdom with which she has carried out her duties are a proof, not of her equality, but of her superiority to men. . . . Is it right, at a time like this, to treat a woman as property or as household furniture and to confine her to the kitchen, knowing nothing except that she has to live all her life behind four walls? A woman has feelings, intelligence, strength and morals like a man, so on what basis do we allow ourselves to deprive her of education, of the right to enjoy what men enjoy, of liberty and of the freedom of movement?[35]

As another young man explained, 'The unjust differentiation between the sexes . . . stems from tradition and customs, born in an ignorant and backward society deprived of the means of progress and civilization.'[36]

On the other hand, women were also considered to be different from men, in the sense that they bear children and are involved in childcare. They are the mothers, housewives, sisters and partners upon whom men depend to bring up their children, have their meals prepared and maintain their houses in an 'elegant' fashion:

> How good it would be if only we could introduce into the present curriculum subjects such as cookery, dressmaking and housekeeping and provide elementary lessons in nursing and childcare. This is not to make

of the Kuwaiti girl an excellent cook or a housewife, but rather to inculcate in her mind a sense of etiquette and of creativity, as well as to teach her how to look properly after her dream home.[37]

The contradictions between these two arguments are inherent in a patriarchal ideology which offers women nothing more than an illusion of liberation. Throughout history, it has been rare for men voluntarily to concede their privileged positions to women; improvements in women's lives have been accepted only so long as they do not jeopardize the asymmetrical gender relations of power. Progressive Kuwaiti men did not want to give women full independence or the right to complete self-determination. The kind of liberation they envisaged was one 'which would uproot backward thought from the Arab mind, in the sense that men and women could walk together towards progress and civilization'.[38]

What these young men wanted was simply to 'modernize' women's lives, that is, to educate women so that they could take up jobs 'as teachers, nurses or doctors in order to replace foreign workers',[39] and more importantly, to get rid of the black *abbaya*, the vestige of a backward and ignorant society. Though many merchant families began to allow their women to drop the veil when travelling abroad, at home it was a different matter. Until 1960 women were not allowed to go to the *suq*, or to the tailor to be fitted for Western-style clothes, or even to be driven around the town in a private car, without being veiled.[40]

The *abbaya* remained tied to the idea of honour and chastity. It has long served to distinguish between respectable and non-respectable women. To discard the *abbaya*, the merchant-class community needed to replace the old symbols of honour and chastity with new ones, in other words, to strip the *abbaya* of its signifiers. This is exactly what the progressive young men attempted to do. One wrote:

> If we look around us in Kuwait or in other countries, we notice that some women are walking in the streets unveiled; does this mean that such women are prostitutes and that they do not have any *karama* [honour]? To be unveiled does not necessarily imply that the woman is a whore. On the contrary, she can be honest and righteous. The *abbaya* hides so many things and, for this reason, it is the cause of so many problems in Kuwait. . . . When a man walks in the street and sees an unveiled woman, he passes with indifference; whereas when he sees a woman wearing the *abbaya*, he stares at her trying to see what is hidden beneath her *abbaya*. A man is curious by nature.[41]

Another man claimed that 'honour is about principles, ideology and personal will; the *abbaya* has nothing to do with the making of a woman's honour.'[42] On the contrary, these young men repeatedly argued, the *abbaya* would allow women to conceal their identity, consequently enabling them to indulge in unlawful acts with men without the knowledge of their families. Henceforth, they claimed, 'being *sufur* [unveiled] is safer for women than wearing the *hijab* [veil]'.[43] It was safer because it would make women more identifiable, and such identification could in itself operate as an instrument of social control, preventing them from speaking to unrelated men on their way to the *suq* simply for fear of being seen.

To be able to see women was also important for the young educated merchant-class men who objected to the traditional marriage system. It was not the arranged marriage itself to which they were opposed, but rather the uneasy marital union between two people who had not met before. They wanted to be able to choose their wives and to assess their characters beforehand.[44] As one wrote:

> We want Kuwaiti girls to rebel against traditions, first and foremost against the black *abbaya*, which inspires depression and grief, so that a young man can see his partner before the beginning of the most difficult experience of his life; also, so that he can speak to her and assess her education, her knowledge, and her understanding of life. . . . We want them to be unveiled so that a young man will not marry a woman without seeing her face.[45]

They did not want to meet just any women, however. All they wanted was to be able to see their own womenfolk and choose one as their bride, calling it *iktilat aili salim* (safe familial mixing between the sexes).[46]

The Rebellion of Merchant-class Women

The young progressive men did not simply write about their aspirations and desires; they went so far as to encourage women to lift their veils and to call for their emancipation. As early as 1950 *al-Ba'tha* had its Rukn al-Mar'a (Women's Corner), a section reserved entirely for women's issues and in which Kuwaiti women were asked to express their views. Soon all Kuwaiti newspapers had a women's column.

Between 1950 and 1960 merchant-class women, all of them in their teens, wrote about 10 articles. There is little in their writings to suggest the existence of a feminist consciousness or an awareness of gender politics. They wrote, albeit inconsistently, about the issues that mattered most to them: in the 1950s, education and the veil and later, in the early 1960s, the employment of women. They showed an eagerness to learn, repeatedly expressing their anger at the absence of a proper education for women. One wrote:

> When the girls' primary school was opened, the first graduates looked with excitement to the Council for Education, hoping that a little attention would be paid to them and that the doors of knowledge would be open to them as they were to men. . . . But that was a dream which did not materialize. . . . If the council had shown a little interest, the girls would by now have obtained their secondary degrees, as five years have elapsed since their graduation. Girls are no less intelligent or less motivated than boys.[47]

It was not until 1952 that secondary-level classes were introduced at two primary schools for girls. But for many young women, this was not enough; they wanted a separate secondary school. They also wished to pursue higher education. They regarded education as the source of future 'happiness' and the key to liberation. They believed Western women to be much happier because they were not veiled and were working side by side with men.[48]

They dealt with the issue of the veil not simply by writing about it but also in a more direct manner. In 1953 a group of merchant-class women held a meeting at one woman's house to discuss the issue of *hijab* and *sufur* and then sent their views to one of the local papers, *al-Ra'id*. The next day *al-Ra'id,* praising their courage, published the following statement:

> For the first time in the history of Kuwait—and in the history of the Arabian peninsula—honourable women from noble families held a private meeting, discussed with sincerity and wisdom what was on their minds, and exposed the issue of *sufur* and *hijab* in a way that would make every intellectual in this country envious. And when *al-Ra'id* registers this important incident in its pages, it is to praise such an act of courage by our noble girls and, once again, to assert—as we have done so many times—that we will remain at war with every sign of backwardness [*rajiya*] which stands against the spread of science and knowledge. So, our Kuwaiti girls, keep moving forward![49]

The merchant-class women did 'move forward' and their protest against the veil took a more radical form. In 1956 four young women took off their *abbaya*s, burnt them in their school yard and returned home unveiled. Hearing about the incident, their parents and the men of the community reacted angrily. The young women were told that if they wished to drop the *abbaya* they must stop going to school. To avoid losing what they cherished most, the next day they returned to school veiled.[50] None the less, the incident led the men of the community to question seriously the issue of *hijab* and *sufur*; for almost three years, it was to dominate the discussions in their *diwaniyas*.[51] About a year later, the Council for Education introduced a new school uniform for girls, consisting of a short black dress with red ribbons, putting an end to the black *abbaya*. For older women, however, the *abbaya* remained the rule and very few could venture outside unveiled.

Educated merchant-class women were determined to drop the *abbaya* completely. During their studies abroad, they did not wear the veil. Their families grew accustomed to seeing them unveiled and were proud of them. They were the first generation of Kuwaiti women to go to university. In 1960, on their return to Kuwait, they refused to put on the *abbaya* even if this meant renouncing their careers. Veiling was obligatory for any woman wishing to work in a government department—even foreign teachers had to wear the veil.[52] But educated merchant-class women did not want to wear the *abbaya*, which they saw as the symbol of backwardness, and this time they had their families on their side. In 1961, faced with growing opposition to the veil and the desire to modernize the country, the government finally gave women permission to work without being veiled.[53]

Having persuaded the men of their community to acknowledge their right to a state of *sufur*, educated merchant-class women now turned their attention to the field of employment. There had hitherto been little opportunity for women: the only available jobs were at the ministries of Health, Education, and Social Affairs and Labour.

In 1961, when the Council for Education decided to restrict women's work to the three ministries, merchant-class women protested publicly.[54] The daughters of the Council's members, who represented the most influential merchant families, met reporters from *al-Hadaf* newspaper to state their opposition. 'With all respect to my father,' said one, 'I am against this decision.' 'My uncle', said another, 'is a member of the Council and I am going to discuss the matter with him.'[55] Some wrote to the papers to express their anger. One merchant-class woman asked:

> Is this [decision] because men are better educated, more knowledgeable and more intelligent than women? If this is the case, what is the use of the diplomas that women get from the best universities, which are similar to those of men, if not better?[56]

In restricting women's work to a few ministries, the Council's intention was to maintain strict segregation between the sexes in the workplace. Their daughters and many other merchant-class women found this utterly unacceptable, given that foreign women were allowed to work in any ministry. 'Does this imply', one asked, 'that foreign women are not *sharifa* [respectable], and is it logical that Kuwaiti women are incapable of preserving their *sharaf* [honour] if they work in government departments?'[57]

The concept of *sharaf* was important for the merchant community. It kept them together and helped them to preserve their privileges. More important, it kept women 'in their place'. Alas, the *nahda* for which they had fought faced them with a new problem: the potential loss of control over women's lives. Merchant-class women were aware of this fear and, since the early 1950s, had repeatedly tried to explain to their families that their liberation would not jeopardize family honour. On the contrary, they argued, this was the kind of liberation which would make them respectable and mean that their country was proud of them.

> The true liberation that we are demanding [one explained] is essential and fair. . . . If a wise person is free and feels responsible for his acts, he will use his freedom in the best manner, keeping himself, as much as possible, away from disgrace, acting with full consciousness and with wisdom.[58]

Perhaps because of such beliefs and the women's sincere willingness to protect their family honour, the Council for Education immediately withdrew its decision. In 1962 two merchant-class women started work at the broadcasting station and others entered the Ministry of Foreign Affairs.

This extraordinary shift from seclusion to paid employment was accompanied by other changes in lifestyle. Women began to drive their own cars and most young married couples moved to their own private houses not far from their families. This new privacy allowed the young merchant-class generation to experience a new form of freedom. They organized parties at which alcoholic drinks were served.

Freeth noted:

> These modern families live in luxuriously furnished houses in the best suburban areas, and entertain in the European way. Although Kuwait state is officially 'dry', in most of their houses the cocktail bar is the most prominent feature of the sitting-room, and there is always a lavish supply of drink. The wife welcomes her guests at the door and moves freely among them. . . . Often at parties there will be dancing to the

record-player, and some Kuwaiti girls, with their husband's consent, will go as far as to partner other male guests.[59]

Occasionally, when they were not tied to family visits and had little to do in the late afternoon, merchant-class women would drive to the Ghazali Club. The club was open to both men and women, and drew much of its clientele from the merchant-class community and the 'sophisticated' foreigners living in Kuwait. With its own dance floor and playing non-stop Western music, it was an exclusive social club. Merchant-class women enjoyed such exclusiveness. They often came to relax after a busy day, to meet friends and chat for hours over a cup of coffee or a soft drink.

The Changing Experiences of Middle- and Lower-class Women

It is often argued that merchant-class women, who were the first to drop the veil, drive a car and work in government departments, set the example for other Kuwaiti women and helped them become emancipated.[60] This may be true for the rising middle class, for the daughters of the *nukhoda*s and a few pearl fishermen who saw new opportunities for wealth and power in the economic changes. These groups were in favour of women's education. But, unlike the wealthy merchant families, they did not send their daughters to college abroad, and the young women had to be satisfied with whatever opportunities were available in Kuwait. Until 1966 there was no university in the country. The highest academic qualification open to middle-class women was a secondary diploma; as a result, they had to take up unqualified jobs, such as receptionists or office workers, or perhaps become primary-school teachers. At this time merchant-class women, who had the privilege of a university education, were entering professional and other more rewarding occupations.

It was not only the educational qualifications and occupations that distinguished merchant-class women from others, but also their lifestyle. Many middle-class women did not wear the *abbaya* at work but had to wear it when they went to the *suq* or other public places.[61] It was only gradually and from the mid-1960s onwards that middle-class women were able to drop the *abbaya* completely. Their lifestyle was less lavish than that of merchant-class women, with whom they had little contact.

As noted in Chapter 1, not all Kuwaitis benefited from the new financial opportunities. Many, like the bedouin and those who lived on the fringes of the old walled town, had little awareness of the new commercial openings. For these people, it seemed as if the *nahda* had never come. Although they became a little wealthier in the sense that they were no longer in debt to the merchants, some could not even afford a television set, the new gadget of the modern society. The older generation were now dependent on the state for assistance and the young, many of whom were illiterate, were employed in the oilfields, or recruited as soldiers or guards for the amir.

Because they earned a regular family income, men of the lower stratum no longer needed to rely on women's work. As a result, the women among this group experienced radical changes in their lives. They were drawn back into the house. Merchant-class women no longer needed their services. Upper-class women now preferred to employ Indian servants, visit professional male tailors in town, and go to hospital for the birth of their children. Midwifery soon became a dying profession.

Furthermore, for lower-stratum women, the loss of their traditional work was not compensated for—as it was in the case of their male relatives—by the availability of more stable jobs. On the contrary, there were no alternatives for them. They were illiterate and were to remain so. Among this social group, the education of women was little valued, perhaps for fear that it would corrupt women and disrupt male authority. In spite of all the government efforts to eradicate illiteracy and impose compulsory education for the age group 6–14, there was growing resistance among this stratum towards the education of women. Women were regarded as useful only as housewives and mothers.

Hence, while the world of merchant-class women was expanding, putting them in contact with Western societies and giving them a new breath of freedom, that of the lower-strata women was shrinking, and the divisions between them widened. Whereas women from different backgrounds had previously been drawn together through the provision of services, with the new economic changes there was little contact between them. Each social group came to lead a totally different and independent existence.

The Growth of the State and its Implications for Women

The oil economy led to a growing importance of the state in controlling women's lives. Health, fertility, education and paid employment, all of which directly affect women, have come under the control of the state, regulated by laws and policies. It is the way these policies have been formulated and their underlying ideology which interests us here. The state, as Moore puts it, 'has a role not just in regulating people's lives but in defining gender ideologies, conception of "femininity" and "masculinity", determining ideas about what sorts of person women and men should be'.[62]

The constitution of the state of Kuwait declares men and women to be equal before the law and guarantees them equal rights to education and paid employment. But equality means the guaranteeing not only of equal rights, but also of equal opportunities for both men and women. In practice, the principle of equality has been absent from state policies. For instance, the Electoral Law denies women the right to vote or to run for election. Such rights are granted only to Kuwaiti men over 20 years of age. Women are not considered eligible 'by nature' to stand for election. In spite of 10 years of campaigning for women's suffrage, the government remains reluctant to modify the Electoral Law. (This issue is discussed further in Chapters 3 and 5.)

On the other hand, the entry of women into the wage-earning sector has been one of the state's main policies. Since the production of oil and the massive influx of foreign labour, the government has acknowledged the importance of Kuwaiti women in the labour force. The First Five Year Plan, for the period 1967/68–1971/72, stated that 'population policy should take into account the need to increase the contribution of Kuwaitis to the total labour force and that this cannot be achieved unless Kuwaiti women are encouraged to enlist in suitable activities'.[63] To facilitate the integration of women into the labour force, women were given similar educational opportunities to men. A growing number of secondary schools for girls and teachers' training institutes were established. Women were admitted to the University of Kuwait and education was made compulsory for all children between the ages of 6 and 14.

However, by educating women, the state was aiming not to broaden their work options, but rather to make use of their skills in certain type of jobs 'which are most suited to the nature of women'.[64] It has always been state policy to restrict the employment of women to gender-specific occupations, rather than to eliminate gender roles. The Five Year Plan for the period 1985/86–1989/90 outlined as an objective of state policy:

> encouraging the participation of Kuwaiti women in occupations which are best suited to their nature, and which, at the same time, help to fill state requirements for labour, particularly in the teaching profession, social work, the medical field with all its branches, and scientific research.[65]

The state has also taken measures to protect women at work. The labour law forbids employers from making women work night shifts, except in hospitals and under certain specified circumstances. Women are also prevented from working in industry or in dangerous and strenuous jobs which could be detrimental to their health. These measures, which are supposedly to protect women, tend 'to confirm structures of inequality' between the sexes and to perpetuate the idea that women are 'weaker' than men and that they are in need of 'protection from certain kinds of work'.[66]

All the policies of the Kuwaiti state are built upon the premise that women are weaker than men and in need of protection. Women are placed under the guardianship of men (husband/father/uncle); it is inconceivable that they could exist without the protection of men and with an identity of their own. They are defined as family members whose rights and obligations are circumscribed by their roles as mothers, wives and daughters. The family has always been an important institution for the state: the constitution refers to it as 'the cornerstone of society' and article 9 proclaims that 'the law shall preserve the integrity of the family and strengthen its ties and protect under its auspices motherhood and childhood'.

To consolidate the institution of the family, the state adopted Islamic Family Law borrowed from the Maliki school of jurisprudence as a means of regulating sexuality, marriage, divorce and inheritance. It is beyond the scope of this book to discuss Islamic Family Law in depth; suffice it to say that, overall, it operates in favour of men. Women are put under the protection of men, whether their husbands or kinsmen. Men are in charge of maintaining the family and women are required to be obedient. Divorce is strictly in the hands of men and no woman has the right to conclude an act of marriage without the consent of her father, who acts as her guardian.

It is in the area of welfare provision that the definition of women as family members has the most devastating implications for women, particularly among lower-income groups. This definition means that welfare payments are made directly to men as heads of families, perpetuating women's dependence upon their husbands and the state. More significantly, it also implies that women cannot receive social benefits unless they are no longer under the protection of men or their families, that is, as widows or divorcees who have no one to support them. Individual women are not entitled to claim state benefits. The state does not recognize women as individuals in their own right but rather as members of families.

Housing policy provides a good example of the way the state discriminates against women. As the housing policy was formulated, it came to benefit the family and men rather than women. State houses are allocated to men as heads of households. If a man remarries, his divorced wife either continues to share the same house or returns to her own family. A divorced wife is not entitled to receive a rent subsidy or to apply for state housing. It is only when she has children, does not intend to remarry and has no one to support her that she can claim a rent allowance. In other words, women need to fulfil certain conditions before being entitled to a place of their own where they can live with their children. The implications of such a policy on women's lives are far-rcaching. The divorce rate in Kuwait is very high: one out of five marriages breaks down. As a result, many divorced women, who have no families to support them and no income, end up living barely above the poverty line. Their allowance from the state is hardly enough to pay the rent and provide for the children. Their ex-husbands, who remain in the spacious state houses with their new wives, very often fail to fulfil their responsibilities towards them.

Thus the entire policy of the state has been designed to perpetuate patriarchal relationships and to maintain the traditional role of women. Not even in employment does the state seek to eliminate the asymmetrical gender relations of dependency. Women are required to perform a dual role, that of mothers and paid workers (see Chapter 5), while being denied basic rights. The importance that the state attaches to children is part of its policy to increase the Kuwaiti population. Financial incentives are provided to encourage young Kuwaitis to get married and to have large numbers of children.

Conclusion

In spite of vast improvements in women's status, the roots of oppression have remained largely the same. Little has changed since the discovery of oil, except perhaps that upper-class women have ceased to be secluded and have been drawn, like many others, into the labour market. Women continue to be defined as mothers, wives and daughters, and to be placed under the authority of men. The state does not simply control women's lives, and take over what was previously the main responsibility of kinsmen; it has gone so far as to prevent women seeking an identity of their own other than that of mother, wife or daughter.

Perhaps what is more alarming is that the divisions between women have been accentuated by the rise of the oil economy. The rich have become richer and the poor have remained powerless. Merchant-class women, because of their class membership, found far greater opportunities than others and soon formed a category apart. To what extent these divisions have affected the rise of a feminist consciousness will be examined in the following chapters.

3
The Early Women's Organizations and the Campaign for Women's Rights

In 1963 two women's societies were established: the Cultural and Social Society* (CSS) and the Arab Women's Development Society (AWDS). For more than a decade, they remained the only organizations to speak and act on behalf of Kuwaiti women. Not only do these early women's groups represent an important phase in the history of the women's movement in Kuwait; they are also essential to our understanding of the contemporary women's societies. The emphasis placed on female domesticity and the rise of religious women's groups in the 1980s are direct consequences of the way the early women's organizations, particularly the AWDS, struggled with the issue of equal rights.

The CSS and the AWDS developed against the background of a male society eager to modernize itself but not ready to make any serious changes in gender relations. In the 1960s merchant-class women began to travel, to study abroad and to work alongside men. Kuwaiti men watched them with a mixture of pride and apprehension. The men's desire to free women from their seclusion remained tied to a deep need to keep them under control. This contradiction between the call for women's emancipation and the need to maintain female subordination became apparent when, in the 1970s, the AWDS began to challenge the male conception of modernity and to call for

*Renamed Women's Cultural and Social Society (WCSS) in 1966.

equal rights and equal opportunities. The male reaction to the AWDS's feminist demands was one of anger and reproach, leading to the demise of the AWDS in 1980.

This chapter is devoted to the CSS (WCSS) and the AWDS. It begins by looking at the reasons behind their formation and at the social status of their members. It then examines the objectives and activities of each society, giving a detailed account of the AWDS's campaign for equal rights and of the reaction it provoked within the society at large. Finally, it looks at the two organizations' relationship with each another, their move towards union and the demise of the AWDS.

So far no attempt has been made, either by scholars or by Arab feminists, to write the history of women's organizations in Kuwait except for a series of books by Nouria al-Sadani, the founder of the AWDS, on her experiences in the society and in the campaign for women's rights. The writing of this chapter has been based entirely on primary sources, from newspaper records to interviews with the leaders.

The Birth of the Women's Societies

By the early 1960s merchant-class women had almost everything they had ever wished for: they dropped the veil, studied at the best foreign universities, took paid employment and drove their own cars. Compared to the experiences of their mothers, such moves were in themselves revolutionary. None the less, these women continued to feel that something was missing in their lives.

Since the early 1950s, when Kuwaiti men began to establish voluntary associations, merchant-class women had cherished the idea of establishing their own society. One woman wrote, 'One of the humble endeavours that we aspire towards is the formation of women's societies and charitable organizations through which we can get in touch with poor women and try to help them.'[1]

In the early 1960s the issue was again raised in the press. 'Let's establish a women's society', one woman wrote, 'to take part in the awakening of women and to supervise and guide young people from well-established families and those from poorer families who lack education and knowledge.'[2] Another commented:

> It has become a necessity to establish a women's society built upon solid ground in order for it to carry out its mission towards the Kuwaiti women; that is, to raise the awareness of backward housewives who do

> not have the privilege of an education and to teach them proper methods of childcare and guide them towards a better social life.[3]

The idea of establishing a women's society was well received by the merchant community. The families even encouraged women to engage in public activities. The real intention behind this encouragement was not to emancipate women as part of the *nahda* movement but rather to give them something 'useful' to do. Among the merchant class, there was a serious concern about family honour. Men feared that women might use their spare time, triggered perhaps by boredom, to indulge in illicit relationships with men. In August 1962 an article appeared in *al-Hadaf* entitled, 'The Danger of Corruption is Threatening Kuwaiti Women! Women's Organizations are Capable of Preventing the Catastrophe.' The article, written by a man, warned against the dangers of Westernization, which could drive Kuwaiti women towards 'the path of corruption':

> If we do not properly direct them [women] towards the right path, they will eventually search for the road which would lead them to this [Western] civilization . . . and there the catastrophe begins . . . deviance and corruption begin! . . .How can we prevent this if we do not fill women's spare time? How can we prevent this when we do not see a single club for girls or a women's society? The women's organizations . . . are the ideal way to prevent deviance.[4]

Encouraged by their families, a group of educated merchant-class women approached the Ministry of Social Affairs and Labour in 1963 to ask about establishing a society for women. Immediately afterwards, they formed the Cultural and Social Society (CSS), wrote its constitution and sent it, along with their names and addresses, to the ministry.

In the same year, a young woman from a middle-class background became interested in setting up a society for women. Her name was Nouria al-Sadani; she was then unaware of the merchant-class women's plan. Al-Sadani was an intermediate student with an enthusiasm for broadcasting. In 1962 she joined the Kuwait Broadcasting Station, where she spent many afternoons as a volunteer. In 1963 she left school and took a full-time job as a broadcaster. There she met several merchant-class women and came into contact with a government official who, when he heard of her wish to establish a women's society, advised her to find members and write a constitution. By her own account, al-Sadani was thrilled at the idea; she rushed to inform the educated merchant-class women, hoping that they would join her in forming a society. Much to her disappointment, her proposition was 'haughtily' turned down. In one of her books, al-Sadani recalls these early days:

> I first went to the graduates, who were very few then and who, after overcoming their astonishment, haughtily and selfishly refused to co-operate with me as I was still an intermediate student, too young for them to accept! . . . That refusal was invaluable to me and opened my eyes to many things. . . . I went to the real people, the middle-class people, who came along with me with all their sincerity, nationalism and faith.[5]

Al-Sadani managed to persuade six young women to join her. Like her, these women did not belong to the privileged merchant class and had not had the opportunity to study in universities abroad. They held secondary diplomas and were working full time in the Ministry of Social Affairs and Labour as technical support workers for the professional staff.[6] Soon after they had met, al-Sadani organized a tea party to celebrate the formation of their society. They called it the Arab Women's Development Society (AWDS), wrote a constitution and submitted it to the Ministry of Social Affairs and Labour.

In 1963 the CSS and the AWDS were both licensed. Soon afterwards, both groups began searching for a headquarters. The AWDS turned for assistance to the Minister of Finance, who ordered the Department of Housing to provide them with a furnished house, an order which was soon executed. Al-Sadani wrote:

> At last the dream became a reality. We had our headquarters. The telephone line was soon installed and the Department of Housing sent the furniture as requested. A few months later, the Ministry of Social Affairs and Labour paid us the government allowance of KD3,000—minus KD750 deducted as a rental charge to the Department of Housing. . . . We then bought a small car and employed a clerk.[7]

The AWDS members moved into their newly built headquarters in 1975 but, as we shall see, their stay was to be brief.

The CSS temporarily rented a house in the newly built area of Keyfan. In 1964 they asked the government to provide them with 20,000 square metres of land on which to build their headquarters, but the government was slow to respond. On 1 August 1967 the society's leaders met with government officials to discuss the issue. The minutes of the meeting read:

> A long discussion centred around the headquarters issue and the members' desire to build a permanent headquarters with the help of the ministry. The society's points of view are that the rent charged for their present headquarters, although only temporary, is far too high and that such a sum of money would be better spent on more useful programmes that would benefit the country; on the other hand, this temporary headquarters is hindering and limiting the society's activities and does not give a true picture of the awakening of Kuwait or of its women. They also pointed out that the present government allowance is not sufficient to allow them to build a suitable headquarters. They requested additional financial assistance from the ministry in order to build a large headquarters similar to that of the Teachers Society and the Social Reform Society. The delegates informed them that the ministry has finally succeeded in securing a large piece of land that would be at their disposal at any moment and that the ministry is willing to assist the society financially in the building of their permanent headquarters. The delegates have also emphasized that the society should not expect the state to finance the whole project and that they ought to think about ways of financing it.[8]

The construction costs of the headquarters were estimated at KD1,500,000.[9] By 1987, after 13 years and despite many charity bazaars to raise funds, the headquarters was still not finished: only the main administrative building had been built. Half of the land, which was reserved for a sports club, remains undeveloped and is surrounded by brick walls.

Contrasting Aspirations (1963-1980)

Throughout the 1960s and well into the mid-1970s, when there was a brief union between the two organizations, the CSS (WCSS) and the AWDS had very few contacts with one another. Each group pursued its own activities based on its own view of the correct role of a women's society. The CSS (WCSS) saw its role specifically in terms of providing entertainment for its members and charity for the poor, whereas the AWDS aimed to modernize society and raise the status of women.

The sharp contrast in ambitions and aspirations between the two women's organizations corresponded with the social status of their members. The CSS (WCSS) provided a social gathering-place for those educated merchant-class women with a comfortable life and a well-paid job who complained of boredom and were wealthy enough to indulge in charity work. For the

AWDS members, however (who nevertheless aspired to be like the merchant-class women: modern and educated), modernizing the community meant providing education and work for women. Gradually, the AWDS began to perceive the existence of a wide gap between the genders: Kuwaiti men had the vote, they had better job opportunities and they were promoted much faster than women. They also had the absolute right to end a marriage. Married women were vulnerable and insecure. There were no nurseries available for working mothers and no jobs or training centres for illiterate women. Following this realization, the AWDS launched its campaign for equal rights in the early 1970s.

The contrast in aspirations of the two women's societies is the subject of the following section, which begins by looking at the WCSS activities before examining the AWDS and its campaign for women's rights.

The Women's Cultural and Social Society

On 5 July 1966 the Ministry of Social Affairs and Labour addressed a letter to the society which read as follows:

> Dear Madam President of the Cultural and Social Society,
> Due to the existence of a society exclusively for men with a name similar to that of your society, that is, 'Cultural and Social Society', and which has often caused confusion as to the correspondence procedures for both societies;
> Therefore, the ministry thinks it important that your society summon its members to an extraordinary meeting in order to consider inserting the word 'women' so as to differentiate it from the aforementioned men's society,
> Please accept, madam, our deepest respects.

A general assembly was called and the members agreed to add the word 'women'. At that point the society came to be known as the Women's Cultural and Social Society (WCSS).

The society had one objective: to help Kuwaiti women find ways to occupy their spare time in a manner that would be useful to them and to the society at large. More precisely, as stated in the constitution, it was 'to provide members with the most outstanding social, cultural and sporting activities'.[10]

In the early days, the WCSS's only commitment was to its members and the leaders did not seek to extend available services to non-members. Membership was restricted to women who knew how to read and write, and who had completed their education. Students were excluded from membership.[11] At a time when illiteracy was widespread and the young female generation that could benefit from universal education had yet to leave school, this meant that only educated merchant-class women could become members of the WCSS.

Indeed, the WCSS was soon to become a kin-based society, with the majority of its members related to one another either through kinship ties or marriage. They were recruited from the most prominent merchant families who controlled the country's major private companies. The press was quick to criticize the WCSS's intention of recruiting only women from merchant-class families. The society's leaders, while admitting this fact ('We do have a number of women from well-known Kuwaiti families'), simply replied, 'Have we rejected anyone?'[12] They had not. But the fact that the organization comprised only the elite was sufficient to discourage lower- and middle-stratum women from participating.

Tea Parties and Social Welfare Activities. The most notable features of the WCSS during the 1960s and 1970s, and which were soon to become its hallmarks, were its tea parties and social welfare activities. From the time it was established, the leaders were committed to providing some kind of entertainment for their members. In 1969 they organised a short trip to the United Arab Emirates, partly for sightseeing and partly to meet their 'Arab sisters.'[13] During their regular tea parties, members entertained themselves with a variety of quizzes and games.

The tea parties should not, however, be seen simply as recreational activities. Like visiting, they serve important social functions by providing an opportunity to consolidate kin relations and, at the same time, maintain cohesive ties among members of the upper strata. They promote class intimacy in the sense that members of a similar class, who are not necessarily kin-related, are drawn together in mutually supportive relationships. Hence, the only outsiders invited to the tea parties were ambassadors' wives and occasionally the wives of visiting officials. Through the years, the relationships between the ambassadors' wives and the WCSS evolved from being 'regular guests' to 'good friends'. As we shall see in Chapter 4, in the early 1980s it was the ambassadors' wives who offered assistance to the WCSS with their cooking classes.

The WCSS was the first organization in Kuwait to introduce the concept of a *suq khairi* (charity bazaar). The idea arose as members searched for ways to raise the funds needed to build their headquarters. At these bazaars, they sold a variety of items from clothes to luxury accessories for a sum left to the discretion of the buyer. The first charity bazaar was held in 1966 under the patronage of the Minister of Social Affairs and Labour. It was attended by a number of officials and wealthy merchants who donated a vast amount of money. The charity bazaar became the most glamorous and highly publicized social event of the year, owing much of its success as a fund-raising activity to the influential position of WCSS members within the power structure of society.

Not all the funds went to subsidize the society's in-house projects; large sums were used to finance charity programmes. Starting in the early 1960s, CSS (WCSS) members became involved in charitable projects that extended beyond national frontiers. In 1966 and 1967 they held three bazaars to support Arab governments in their war against Israel. In 1969 they began to send funds on a regular basis to an orphanage in Palestine. A few years later, the WCSS helped to finance the building of an orphanage in Lebanon.

In the winter, WCSS members distributed warm clothes to low-income families. They also paid regular visits to the Children's Home (Dar al-Tufula), which cared for orphans and children from broken homes. There, they entertained the children and gave them toys and other gifts. On national holidays, they visited several hospitals to distribute gifts to patients.

Apart from providing charity, the WCSS did little to improve the lives of lower-class women. In 1966, during their 'Keep Kuwait Tidy' campaign, they lectured lower-class women on the virtues of hygiene and cleanliness, but made no attempt to respond to their social problems.

On 15 December 1971, in an interview with the press, the WCSS president, Lulua al-Qitami, was asked whether the society should help less privileged women, such as 'those who are on the edge of committing suicide because they are finding it impossible to communicate with their illiterate parents and those who get beaten by their husbands'. Her answer was:

> I suppose what they should do is to contact the Ministry of Social Affairs and Labour where there is a whole department in charge of family problems. This department has specialists who devote their time to doing social work. It is impossible for our society to follow these kinds of problems. We do not have a sufficient number of ladies who could devote their time to these issues. I also think that television should present educational programmes to help in solving these problems; and, because almost every house has a television set, the effect will be much more powerful.[14]

Seeing that the WCSS leaders were so clearly uninterested in their problems and experiences, many Kuwaiti women who were not part of the upper class began to lose hope in the organization. The WCSS leaders made no attempt to attract these women to their society.

Cultural Debates and Women's Issues. Whether for lack of ideas or of volunteers, the WCSS held very few cultural seminars. They took place infrequently and subjects were chosen for their topicality rather than because of any intrinsic interest. For instance, in 1964, when a deputy raised the question of women's suffrage in the National Assembly, the CSS immediately organized a public debate to discuss the issue. At the end of the debate, no resolutions were adopted or recommendations made.[15] The leaders did not take the debate much further. The issue was soon forgotten and for two years the CSS did not hold another public debate. It was not until 1966 that the society held a few seminars on the issues of childcare and youth problems. Then the seminars stopped, to begin again in the mid-1970s.

In 1965 CSS leaders attended a symposium on motherhood and childcare held in Cairo. Two years later, they accepted an invitation to attend the celebrations held on the occasion of International Women's Day in the Soviet Union, of which they said, 'WCSS's participation has shown the world the *nahda* [awakening] of Kuwaiti women and has strengthened the ties with outside women's organizations.'[16]

It was not until the mid-1970s that WCSS leaders became more involved in women's issues. This involvement did not stem from a genuine interest in women but rather from a concern over women's role in society. At that time, the government was beginning to pressure the women's societies 'to review their objectives' and to become more involved in social work. The government's argument was that it was the reponsibility of all citizens to serve the country in return for the services they were receiving. The women's organizations were accused of not 'serving their country' and of not 'doing something that could be useful to the society at large.'[17]

For this reason, in 1975, in collaboration with the government, the WCSS undertook a survey of the factors preventing illiterate women from attending adult literary classes. In the same year, they set up a small tailoring enterprise which aimed to help lower-class women earn a meagre living. The scheme lasted less than a year because it failed to attract enough women. In 1975 the society also established a nursery, which quickly expanded: by 1980 it had 10 large classrooms, a cafeteria and an outdoor playground. By 1987 the nursery was run by 18 qualified staff members who each received a salary of KD120 per month. Between 1975 and 1987 the number of children admitted to the nursery increased from 14 to 175. The factors behind the establishment of the nursery are discussed in detail in Chapter 5.

The UN declaration of the Decade for Women (1976–85) and the Kuwaiti government's growing interest in women's organizations playing an official role at international conferences led the WCSS to rethink its objectives. The president took the role of an official delegate, becoming a 'femocrat whose job is to speak officially on behalf of women'.[18]

In 1975, in collaboration with male Arab scholars, the WCSS sponsored the first Regional Conference on Women in the Arabian Gulf. Although delegates from various women's associations in Arab countries participated, all the papers were presented by male scholars. At the close of the conference, a series of recommendations were issued that were somewhat similar to those of the AWDS:

1. to involve women in the drafting of the family law;
2. to grant women their political rights;
3. to promote equal employment opportunities;
4. to involve women in national development; and
5. to press the government to ratify all international legislation pertaining to women.[19]

The WCSS considered women's suffrage and equality in employment to be the major issues for Kuwaiti women. In the 1970s, however, WCSS members made little effort to promote women's rights. In sponsoring the Regional Conference on Women, the WCSS was, at the time, mainly responding to the UN's declaration of the Decade for Women.

The Arab Women's Development Society

The AWDS adopted a different approach from the WCSS. It did not seek to fulfil the aspirations, either cultural or social, of its individual members. Instead, more general women's issues were central to the AWDS. From its inception, its leaders aimed to 'modernize' women, firmly believing that education was the key to their liberation. Later, as they came into contact with Arab feminist groups, the AWDS leaders realized that if the position of women was to change, society had to alter its attitude and enforce legislation which would promote and guarantee gender equality. They held many conferences to bring women together and to raise their awareness of gender discrimination. In 1973 an Equal Rights Bill was put before the National Assembly, provoking the most stormy debate in its history. It is this shift from the concept of modernization to that of equal rights which we shall focus on in the following pages.

'Modernizing' Women. In 1963 the AWDS set itself a number of objectives, orienting its activities accordingly. These objectives were:

1. to serve the individual, the family, the community and the country;
2. to encourage social, health, educational and welfare projects;

3. to promote the cultural and educational advancement of Kuwaiti women and to call for women's rights;
4. to promote women's activities in all kinds of fields (i.e. social, scientific and cultural);
5. to find remedies for all kinds of social problems;
6. to teach Kuwaiti women foreign languages;
7. to follow the progress of women in Arab and foreign countries and to support their activities as well as to introduce them to the activities of Kuwaiti women; and
8. to promote public awareness of the importance of the family in society.[20]

These objectives, which aimed to promote the involvement of women in the public sphere, to 'enlighten' the uneducated and to preserve family order, reflected the prevailing male desire to 'modernize' Kuwait.

As noted earlier, the idea of modernizing the country began to spread soon after the discovery of oil. Modernization, often equated with *nahda* (progress), meant raising the educational standard of the population, involving women in the economic sphere and using modern technology. The modernization discourse, which drew its models from the West, offered a simplified vision of the world, which was portrayed as divided between two contrasting types of society: the 'backward' and the 'civilized'.

AWDS members, who took a genuine interest in the lives and experiences of women, were deeply influenced by the male view of civilization. They also regarded traditional customs as backward and 'outdated', and felt they ought to be replaced by more modern, 'civilized' customs. The *nahda* was believed to be the key to the liberation of Kuwaiti women. Education, perceived as fundamental to any civilization, would liberate women from the state of 'ignorance' to which they had long been condemned and enable them to participate with men in the building of a civilized society.

The AWDS strongly believed that women could only become truly liberated through education. To this end, throughout the 1960s, they struggled to 'enlighten' women about the importance of education. It was a struggle to which AWDS members committed themselves fully. In a speech delivered during the early days of the society, Nouria al-Sadani explained:

> We cannot solve the problems of women or liberate them by writing on paper or by endless discussion of their rights. We have to work, toil patiently and create conditions for their liberation so that they may move quickly enough to catch up with the procession of women in the countries that are ahead in civilization. . . . Our society has the sacred duty and

> noble aim of promoting the status of women and achieving a fair deal for them as compared with men, so that women may stand with men in all fields of life. . . . How painful and depressing it is for us to see half of the community stagnating in the house under the pressure of stone-hard minds greatly damaged by the effects of time, circumstances, customs and traditions, and as a result having not a glimpse of enlightenment.[21]

In the early 1960s the Women's Enlightenment Committee (a sub-committee of the AWDS) was formed. Its aim was to raise the status of bedouin women and teach them ways of improving their lives. In 1967 the committee members visited the village of Jahra to give a lecture on the role of women in the community. The bedouin women simply did not attend. When the committee members arrived at the place reserved for the lecture, they found nobody there, only empty chairs. But al-Sadani and her colleagues decided not to give up and headed for the nearest school. They made the trip on foot, at night, and in bad weather. When they finally reached the school, they interrupted the evening classes and gave the lecture to an audience of about 200 bedouin women.

The lecture was followed by a film on the stages of child-rearing that lasted for nearly two hours. Al-Sadani, who gave the lecture,[22] spoke in rather patronizing tones. She told the bedouin women that they ought to change their 'traditional bad manners that are now outdated'. She explained that first they needed to keep their low-income houses 'in good order rather than attach ugly huts to them, which create an ugly appearance and an unhealthy place to live'. As for interior decoration, they should 'refer to women's magazines for ideas and learn how best to run the house'. Second, whether married or unmarried, young or old, they should all attend the local schools in order to be trained for jobs. They should encourage their daughters 'to enrol in various school activities so that they can develop their talents and occupy their minds with useful things'.

Third, al-Sadani said, they must look after their children properly, preventing them from playing barefoot in dusty roads 'because that may lead to very serious diseases', and helping them to organize their time between study and play 'so that they grow accustomed to being organized'. Fourth, they should discard 'primitive methods of cure' and instead seek proper medical advice. Finally, they should keep a harmonious atmosphere in the family: if, for instance, 'a dispute arises between husband and wife . . . the wisest behaviour would be to solve the dispute in order to avoid the breakdown of the family' as a divorce 'would harm the children and disturb their minds; they would grow up deprived of maternal affection'. She concluded:

> We must, therefore, endure and make sacrifices for the sake of our children, and keep our family firmly united. All I pray for is that we safeguard our family life because we thereby safeguard our community, which in turn means to safeguard the fatherland—the major duty in our life.[23]

Al-Sadani apparently intended this lecture to transform the bedouin woman into that new model of 'modern', 'enlightened' woman who participates in the public sphere, who knows how to keep her home clean and tidy and how to look after her children's education, who is wise and obedient, and who sacrifices her life to safeguard her family. It is not known how the bedouin women responded to this neatly dressed and condescending lecturer from the city who spoke of their customs as backward and outdated, nor how they responded to her suggestions, which had no relevance to their everyday problems. However genuine she might have been in her desire to improve the lives of these women, al-Sadani made the same mistake as many Arab modernists: she disregarded tradition and customs in order to speed up the process of modernization.

The emphasis placed on the unity of the family as a means to cement patriotism should not, however, be understood as a central issue for the AWDS. Perhaps because they felt indebted to the government for their existence as an organization, AWDS members were receptive to the state's needs and eager to prove their loyalty. In 1968, when the government called for a Conference on the State of the Kuwaiti Family, the AWDS promptly answered the call and prepared a paper on the issues of divorce and polygamy, which they considered to be the most serious social problems. They saw the main causes of divorce as the breakdown of communication between spouses, and irresponsible behaviour such as the wife neglecting her husband or the husband staying out of the house for too long, treating his wife as 'a piece of furniture'. Such behaviour, they argued, could be prevented through counselling, 'cultural enlightenment', education and an increase in family income.[24]

Interestingly, it was the merchant-class model of a working woman that the AWDS wanted to disseminate, that is, the educated professional woman dutifully participating in the building of her country, a model which not only obscured but also denigrated the existence of the illiterate manual worker. Nor were female manual workers remembered or honoured on 23 February 1970, when a lavish reception (to which a number of government officials were invited) for the First Kuwaiti Women's Day was held to honour the 'vanguard' Kuwaiti women.

The purpose of the celebrations was to promote the idea that women should work to serve the country. Five Kuwaiti women were awarded the Kuwaiti Women's Medal: Moudi al-Ubaidi (a poetess), Fatima al-Shatti (the first woman to work in the Department of Health in 1970), Mariam al-Saleh (the first female teacher), Fatima Hussein (one of the first female university graduates) and Dr Najeeba al-Mulla (the first female doctor). Al-Sadani explained that they deserved to be honoured not only because they were the first to serve their country but also because they set a 'good example' for others. On this occasion, the AWDS published a book entitled *Kuwaiti Women in the Past and Present* which glorified the lives and experiences of upper-class women. It was hoped that this lavish celebration would encourage more Kuwaiti women to enter the professions and would inspire mothers to stress the importance of their children's education.

While wanting women to enter paid employment, AWDS leaders were also aware that women needed first to free themselves from childcare responsibilities. In the 1960s not all women could afford a maid, and there were no childcare facilities. For this reason, in 1967, the AWDS opened the first nursery in Kuwait, which was a great relief for many working mothers. Four years later, the nursery was expanded and equipped with many recreational facilities.[25]

The Equal Rights Issue. In the early 1970s the AWDS began to shift its concern from the issue of modernizing women to that of understanding what Kuwaiti women really wanted. This shift meant a departure from a male approach centred round restructuring women's lives to a feminist perspective of women's rights; it began to crystallize as early as 1964 following the AWDS's affiliation to the Arab Feminist Union (AFU). The union had been formed in 1944 by Huda Shaarawi, a leading Egyptian feminist, who campaigned for the education and enfranchisement of women and for reforms in Islamic Family Law.

Contact with the AFU during conferences abroad was decisive for the AWDS in refining and redefining its notions of equality and rights. In 1971, at the seventh AFU Conference held in Tunis, Arab feminists issued a series of recommendations related to the rights of Arab women and elected Nouria al-Sadani as head of the Arab Family Committee.[26] For al-Sadani, this election meant affirmation of her role in the leading Arab feminist movement and gave her organization a valuable and, in some ways enviable, credibility among Kuwaiti women.

Her new leadership position within the AFU, combined with her deep admiration for Huda Shaarawi, prompted al-Sadani to organize a Kuwaiti Women's Conference on 15 December 1971. The response was overwhelming: 100 women participated; professionals and housewives, wealthy and middle-class women, all mingled together. There was a sizeable number of educated merchant-class women who felt alienated by the repetitive and philanthropic nature of the WCSS, and who looked to the AWDS to formulate a more radical feminist challenge.

This was the first conference to be held in Kuwait exclusively for and by women. It provided a forum for Kuwaiti women to express their feelings and discuss issues related to their own experiences as mothers, housewives and paid workers. They spoke of their dissatisfaction with government policies which denied them equal rights with men in employment and education. Furthermore, they expressed the need for childcare facilities and family planning centres. They also wanted co-education and the eradication of female illiteracy. At the close of the conference, the participants unanimously agreed to put their grievances in writing to the National Assembly. Thereafter, two committees were formed to draw up a petition which was to include seven demands:

1. the unconditional right to contest elections;
2. equality in all fields of employment and greater opportunities for women to reach the highest administrative posts;
3. equality in employment at the Ministry of Foreign Affairs and the enrolment of women in the diplomatic corps;
4. the provision of all allowances for women working in the government sector, including child allowances, which were granted to married men working in the private sector;
5. the appointment of women as special attornies to draft the family law;
6. the restriction of polygamy by stipulating that the second marriage contract must be signed in court; and
7. barring the husband from any child allowance for his second marriage if his first wife had a child.[27]

To justify these demands, they articulated their arguments around the concepts of patriotic duties and citizenship rights, carefully presented within the framework of the Kuwait constitution. They began by arguing that, because of the small size of the Kuwaiti population, the government should use every available human resource to build the nation; the female population constituted an important category in terms of both numbers and potential which could neither be ignored nor removed from the process of national development. Furthermore, they argued that the constitution granted equality and justice to all citizens, male and female alike. Article 41 stipulated that:

> Every Kuwaiti has the right to work and to choose the type of work. Work is the duty of every citizen, necessitated by personal dignity and the public good. The state shall endeavour to make it available to all citizens and to make its terms equitable.

The committee members also pointed out that the constitution stipulated that the 50 members of the National Assembly 'shall be elected directly by universal suffrage and secret ballot in accordance with the provisions presented by Electoral Law'. But, they argued, Kuwaiti women had been denied all their constitutional rights. Not only were they not given access to employment that was equal or similar to men's, but they were also deliberately kept at the bottom of the promotion ladder whereas their male colleagues could expect rapid promotion. Besides, the Electoral Law had reversed the provisions of 'universal suffrage' by excluding women—only men were allowed to participate in the elections.

As to the restriction on polygamy, the women justified their demand in terms of the need to preserve the unity of the family. They argued that the preservation of the family is the duty of mothers as well as fathers. The family is the basic and essential unit of society and should therefore be preserved. The restriction on polygamy was meant to prevent family disintegration and preserve first marriages.

The Debate on Polygamy and Women's Suffrage. The Equal Rights Bill was shelved for almost two years before being considered, in 1973, by the National Assembly's Grievances Committee and put to the Assembly for discussion. During this time, the government began to ease the employment restrictions on women. Kuwaiti women were now allowed to enter the legal profession and work in any of the departments of the Ministry of Foreign Affairs, and promotion opportunities in all kinds of jobs were extended to women. Thus the Assembly focused on two issues: the enfranchisement of women and restrictions on polygamy. The government found these two demands rather embarrassing to deal with; it preferred to leave them to the Assembly for discussion, hoping that at the end of the debate, a motion would be moved to refer the petition to the Assembly's Legal Affairs Committee for thorough study, thus avoiding a formal vote.[28]

As expected, these demands provoked the most stormy debates in the history of the National Assembly. A *Kuwait Times* reporter noted:

> The tension reached a climax yesterday when the speaker declared a half-hour recess in a bid to bring order back to the House, which had plunged into complete chaos. Supporters and opponents of the bill exchanged the

> most hurtful charges ever heard in the Assembly. The recess, instead of calming tempers, increased them because the two groups fought it out in the lounge.[29]

It was the issue of polygamy which caused such fury and anger among the deputies. Opponents of the bill, who formed a majority, argued that any restriction on the practice of polygamy was against the precepts of the Shari'a, the main source of legislation in Kuwait; and that they, as dutiful Muslims, were opposed to any kind of change that would contradict or erode the tenets and precepts of Islam. 'Wouldn't it be better for a woman', argued one deputy, 'to live as a second wife than as a concubine, or a mistress, or in an illegal relationship with a man?'

These deputies claimed that Islam honoured women, bestowing upon them a dignified status and giving them the right to own property, enter into business transactions and keep their maiden name after marriage. But, they insisted, Islam did not make women *equal* to men; in inheritance, for example, a woman's share is half that of her male siblings. Men and women are different. They are given different responsibilities which complement each other. The main duties of a woman are to be a mother and a housewife. It is the husband's duty alone to earn a living and maintain his family. Besides, those women who needed to work should wear modest clothes and avoid mixing freely with men.

The liberation of women, it was argued, did not mean wearing mini-skirts, driving a car or being a paid worker, in other words, 'blindly imitating Western women'. Islam laid down the principles of women's liberation within a context of respect and dignity. Under Islam, it was further argued, women are protected from being reduced to a 'cheap commodity' as in Western societies and are entrusted with the most fundamental duty, that of motherhood. A famous *hadith*, as one deputy reminded the others, runs, 'Paradise is under the feet of mothers.' Therefore, as another deputy argued:

> We [men] ought to choose what is best for her environment and would be in harmony with our true traditions and Islamic civilization. . . . And if we want to honour a woman and preserve her honour, we ought to make her the lady of the house, in charge of the household and of raising the new generation. For this reason, we want to keep her away from the world of politics.[30]

The deputies' insistence on the absolute preservation of Arab–Islamic traditions and respect for the teachings of the Prophet as laid down in the Quran and *hadith* was essentially to prevent what they most feared: the disintegration of the patriarchal system. They were horrified at the idea of equality between men and women:

> To civilize a woman and let her dominate; then women and ourselves become equal! We [men] then become nothing![31]

> Should we struggle to allow women to behave imperiously? Women have dignity and certain rights, but this does not mean that we should give them rights which *do not belong* to them.[32] [Emphasis added]

The deputies' speeches contained many such expressions of anguish at the possibility of women's autonomy, which was perceived as a defiant act and a threat to the indisputable authority of men. They argued that Islam gave men authority over women—men are the 'protectors' of women; women should be obedient to men and should not 'adorn themselves'. Any kind of disobedience on the part of women towards men was considered a direct challenge to Islam:

> Should men be subordinate to women or women be subservient to men? I am asking you, does Islam allow this?[33]

> Why shouldn't we *protect our religion*? We want to protect our religion, but by what rights do these demands impose an order upon men?[34]

> We ought to preserve our heritage and our religion and maintain our beliefs. In Islam, it is men who support women and not women who support men. For this reason, I ask all members of the National Assembly . . . to return to their religion, morality and traditions.[35]

> Women have no right to adorn themselves or to rebel against their obedience to men.[36]

> I disagree with those who say that we ought to give women total freedom. There is a difference between the rights of women and total freedom. Indeed, there is a vast difference. We do welcome and respect women. We also want to give them the right to stand in all fields [of work] side by side with men, but we shall *never* give them total freedom.[37] [Emphasis added]

The bill's supporters were the nationalists and the few liberal-minded merchants who had at least one daughter involved in the women's rights campaign. It should be noted that the former persistently emphasized that the principal role of every woman was to be a housewife and 'to bring up a useful and healthy future generation',[38] that women should not adorn themselves and that Arab–Islamic traditions must be dutifully respected and preserved. But, like the liberal merchants, the nationalists also argued that Kuwaiti women had obtained university degrees and had proved that they were capable of handling public responsibilities, so why should they not be given at least the right to vote when Islam itself did not forbid them from political participation? The nationalists, however, went further by claiming that there could be no true democracy in Kuwait unless freedom of expression and the right to vote were guaranteed for all individuals, men and women alike.

The debate was inconclusive. The Assembly avoided voting on the bill and the discussion ended as it had begun, with bitter resentment between deputies, political rifts and total confusion as to how to define and circumscribe the rights of women. A few months later, that session of the Assembly came to a close and the campaign for the next Assembly began. The nationalist groups adopted the women's rights issues as part of their electoral programme, campaigning for the enfranchisement of women and for equal employment opportunities.[39]

But though it was clothed in the principles of democracy and social justice, their campaign did not at any time proclaim the existence of an absolute equality between the sexes. Rather, it carefully emphasized that equality between men and women must be understood in 'relative terms', for each sex is biologically different and has different roles as prescribed by Islam.[40] Like their opponents, the nationalists were not in favour of greater freedom for women; nor did they want to concede all men's privileges to women or put an end to women's subordination.

The Campaign for Equal Rights. During the hearings, women activists led a campaign to express their views and mobilize public support. They organized public meetings, attended the Assembly sessions, met with government officials and wrote articles in local newspapers. Al-Sadani wrote in *al-Siyassah* newspaper under the pseudonym 'Daughter of the Sun'. The Kuwait National Union of Students (KNUS) invited her to give a talk at the university and organized a public debate on the issue of women's suffrage.

Not all Kuwaiti women supported the equal rights campaign. Those who disagreed, many of whom were from the merchant class, expressed their views in the daily press, dismissing the movement as 'political chaos' and advising women to keep quiet and wait until the time was right.[41] These views were echoed by the Social Reform Society. In April 1973 the society invited Zaynab al-Ghazali, a well-known Islamic activist, to speak about women's rights and duties in Islam.

The fact that women were themselves divided on the equal rights issues had little effect on the campaign. Women activists successfully publicized their cause through various communication media, presenting themselves as a united front to such an extent that the claims of their opponents passed almost unnoticed. In addition, the nationalists' support gave greater weight to their campaign. As noted earlier, the nationalist groups were at that time politically powerful. In 1973 they issued a statement in support of the Equal Rights Bill and held many public debates on the issue.

In February 1974 the AWDS organized a Conference on the Status of Working Women to which a number of officials and a group of women activists were invited. The three-day conference provided an opportunity for middle-class women to put forward their grievances. They issued a series of recommendations which were mainly directed at improving their own status at work. Unlike merchant-class women, they were the most affected by employment legislation and suffered greater discrimination. They did not hold university degrees which would enable them to occupy professional posts. On the contrary, many had only a secondary diploma and therefore had fewer job opportunities. They had several demands:

1. the formation of a permanent committee to be attached to the Council of Ministers under the name, Women's Affairs Committee;
2. the involvement of women in the drafting of legislation pertaining to the family and to women;
3. the setting up of technical training centres for women with secondary diplomas or lower qualifications to increase their chances of finding a job;
4. the establishment of state-run nurseries to encourage women to work;
5. encouragement for women to work for the youth police and the intelligence service;
6. rewards for those working in social welfare institutions;
7. a ban on transferring working women's social allowances to their husbands upon marriage;
8. flexible working hours for teachers;
9. research into the causes preventing women from being promoted;
10. encouragement for women to join trade unions; and
11. a trade union for female employees to promote their interests.[42]

Although these demands were put to the government, legislative reforms were not introduced. Nevertheless, the AWDS continued to press its claims.

In 1974, when a draft of the Personal Family Law was submitted to the National Assembly, the AWDS held a one-week seminar in which a number of male specialists and a group of professional women participated. They proposed amendments to a number of articles which curtailed women's rights. They demanded that the age of marriage be set at 18 or above to prevent young women being forced into arranged marriages; they also demanded that a woman be given the right to marry the man of her choice, to seek a divorce through a court of law and to retain custody of her children after separation.[43]

A year later, the AWDS organized a second Kuwaiti Women's Conference. At a time when the government was redefining its policies towards women's societies, the AWDS leaders preferred to play it safe. They organized the conference under the title, 'The Duties and Rights of Kuwaiti Women within the Context of Global Development'. Four recommendations were issued:

1. to grant women the right to political participation;
2. to adopt the AWDS's amended version of the Family Law;
3. to establish educational centres to eliminate illiteracy and educate the family; and
4. to preserve traditional bedouin crafts.[44]

Immediately after the conference, a group of merchant-class women established Sadu House (Bait al-Sadu) to preserve bedouin crafts and to generate an income for bedouin women.

In 1974 the Kuwaiti Women's Union (KWU) was formed as the sole representative of Kuwaiti women. The KWU aimed to unite the two women's societies and co-ordinate their activities. In August 1976 the government dissolved the National Assembly. The dissolution brought a temporary end to the debate on women's suffrage; it was not revived until 1982, when a bill was presented by one of the deputies, Ahmad al-Takheim, without prior consultation with the women's societies. (For a further discussion of women's suffrage, the reader is referred to Chapter 5.)

In 1977 the AWDS organized a second Conference on the Status of Working Women, where papers were presented and discussed by a group of male experts and professional women. The major recommendations of the conference were the establishment of state-run nurseries, the provision of social allowances for married women and the involvement of women in the formulation of legislation. Two years later, the government appointed two women attorneys in the Department of Jurisprudence and Legislation (al-Fatwa wa al-Tashri).

Divided Women and the End of the AWDS

The relationship between the WCSS and the AWDS had always been characterized by mistrust and undeclared hostility. From the very beginning, WCSS members kept their distance, graciously declining any invitations and not returning offers of collaboration. They saw the AWDS as their competitors and rivals rather than as a group of women with whom they were linked by common experiences of oppression.

Until the late 1960s the WCSS president, Lulua al-Qitami, was regularly in the news giving details of WCSS activities. Throughout this period, she felt neither threatened by nor concerned at the presence of the AWDS. Her society received just as much public attention as the AWDS. More important, its membership consisted of the elite women of Kuwait. When, in 1967, WCSS members were approached by government delegates to explore the possibility of forming a Kuwaiti Women's Union, they weakly replied that they needed to think about it. The government wished to co-ordinate the activities of the two women's societies, amalgamating them into one association which would become the sole representative of Kuwaiti women abroad.

By the early 1970s the situation had changed. The AWDS was in the limelight and had attracted a number of merchant-class women. Never before had the WCSS felt so abandoned by the public and the media. In 1973 one paper printed a cynical remark: 'Where is the society of Lulua al-Qitami? Nouria al-Sadani has taken over the public domain and asserted her presence!'[45]

Few WCSS members joined the women's rights campaign; indeed, many opposed it. This was not because they did not believe in equal rights. On the contrary, as we shall see later, from the late 1970s onwards the WCSS was to stand firmly as an advocate of women's suffrage. What the WCSS leaders were fighting was another women's organization which they saw as stealing a show which should have been theirs.

The WCSS had long cultivated its reputation and its character of 'exclusivity'. As we have seen earlier, its constitution excluded illiterate women from membership. As a result, it became a kin-based society, composed of women from 'well-known families'. Once the AWDS had widened its support base and recruited merchant-class women, however, the 'exclusive' character of the WCSS became more elusive.

In 1974 the AWDS president approached the WCSS to form an association as a way of uniting the two women's societies and harmonizing their activities. She had made a similar attempt in the past but failed, as the WCSS had been reluctant to form a union with the AWDS. This time, al-

Sadani hoped that the popularity of the AWDS and its campaign for women's rights might inspire the WCSS to rethink its policies. Her move was successful: in December 1974 the Kuwaiti Women's Union (KWU) was born,[46] with al-Sadani elected president. Although the board of directors included members from the two women's societies, the election was seen as a victory for the AWDS.

The board was, however, unable to establish a coherent programme of action through which women could secure their political rights and improve their status. There was disagreement on several issues. Each board member continued to represent her own society, rather than speak on behalf of the KWU. In 1975 the WCSS sent its own delegate to the UN World Conference on Women held in Mexico City, much to the surprise of the KWU board, which decided to ignore the matter mainly to avoid stirring up further conflict and schism between the members of the two societies.[47]

Faced with increasing difficulties and frustations, al-Sadani planned to form a third women's society with which the AWDS could ally itself so that together they could exercise a real influence within the KWU. She contacted a group of merchant-class women who had campaigned for women's rights and who equally resented the WCSS's quest for power. Together, they drew up a constitution for the new society and selected its members, mainly from the al-Qinaie family. The society, which was named the Girls Club, had the following objectives:

1. to occupy members' spare time with useful social, cultural and sports activities;
2. to work towards finding appropriate means which would enable members to engage in their hobbies;
3. to consolidate and strengthen the spirit of co-operation between the club and other public associations;
4. to participate in national events by undertaking various social activities;
5. to strengthen family ties by allowing children to take part in the club's sporting activities;
6. to support the charitable organizations of Kuwait; and
7. to increase public awareness of the importance of kinship solidarity and of its implications for the whole society.[48]

In 1976, soon after it was licensed, the Girls Club submitted an application for membership to the KWU. Article 6 of the KWU constitution specified that affiliation to the union could occur only one year after the date of a society's founding. As the Girls Club had only recently been founded, the application was temporarily postponed.

The leaders of the Girls Club and the AWDS turned to the government for support, requesting that article 6 of the KWU constitution be removed. On 25 April 1976 the Ministry of Social Affairs and Labour urged the KWU to summon its members to an extraordinary meeting to consider omitting article 6 of the constitution in order to allow the Girls Club to enter the union. At the meeting, the WCSS members voted against the proposition, while the AWDS members voted to delete article 6. According to the KWU constitution, if there is a tie vote, the president can cast the deciding vote. Al-Sadani did so. As a result, the Girls Club was admitted to KWU membership.

The admission of the Girls Club provoked fury among WCSS members. They were no longer able to cope with a situation where they had lost control; not only had they lost the KWU leadership, they had also been isolated within the union. Feeling powerless, the WCSS decided to quit the KWU. On 12 June 1976 the WCSS leaders addressed a letter to the government, offering their resignation from the KWU. The government's attempt to convince WCSS members to drop their resignation 'in the public interest' was doomed to failure. The WCSS refused categorically to withdraw its decision.

After the departure of the WCSS from the KWU, the government was unsure whether to retain the union or dissolve it. The women's societies were more divided than ever. The KWU, which had been founded specifically to unite and co-ordinate the activities of the women's organizations, appeared unable to overcome the feelings of rivalry and hostility. On 27 April 1977 the government issued a resolution dissolving the KWU.

The demise of the KWU irrevocably deepened the gap between the two women's societies. The Girls Club was soon preoccupied with establishing itself as an all-inclusive sports and social club, searching for an 'appropriate' headquarters large enough to be equipped with all the most popular outdoor sports facilities, such as a swimming pool, basketball court, tennis courts, and so on. Although members of the Girls Club were grateful to al-Sadani as their founder, they maintained a vague and distant relationship with the AWDS after the KWU's dissolution.

Having lost the support of both women's societies, al-Sadani became involved with a men's political group called the Free Democrats (al-Dimuqratiun al-Ahrar), which held political meetings at the AWDS headquarters.[49] The Free Democrats were lobbying for social justice, freedom and democracy, concepts which did not tie in with government policies. Al-Sadani was not, however, politically engaged. Her association with the Free Democrats had started back in the early 1970s when the group defended the Equal Rights Bill. In allowing the group to use the AWDS headquarters for their meetings, she was simply returning a favour.

Al-Sadani remained loyal to the government and was unable to extricate herself from the cult of patriotic duty that she had been professing for so long. Despite this loyalty, the government was quick to exploit any trivial administrative or personal problems within the AWDS in order to justify its long-awaited closure. When, in 1978, a quarrel arose between members over a financial issue, the government immediately sent in an investigator. The AWDS was charged with financial fraud, an accusation which has never been adequately investigated or proven. Al-Sadani was removed from the AWDS leadership and forced into exile. She went to the United Arab Emirates where she became president of the Arab Family Organization (AFO). The AWDS presidency was handed over to a female government official, but AWDS members declined all involvement in its activities and the organization was soon dissolved. On 15 November 1980 the government issued a resolution to close the AWDS. Neither the Girls Club nor the WCSS protested.

In 1980, on the verge of resigning from her duties as president of the AFO, al-Sadani returned to Kuwait intending to set up her own women's organization. Gathering a group of women, she formed the Kuwaiti Women's Society on 23 February 1981. But the application for a licence was rejected in the following words:

> Since there are already two societies for women, the ministry does not, for the time being, see any need for an additional women's society . . . The applicants could exercise their activities by means of affiliation to any of the existing women's societies.[50]

Less than a year later, two Islamic women's societies were licensed.

Now on the periphery of the women's rights movement, al-Sadani was to lead a painful, solitary struggle for a few more years, delivering lectures here and there on women's rights issues before finally retiring bitterly from the public scene.

Conclusion

The struggle for power, coupled with long-standing class rivalries, set Kuwaiti women apart from each other. Through their protracted in-fighting, they jeopardized their autonomy as a group of women with shared experiences. As both victims and oppressors, women were unable to extricate themselves from their loyalties to either their own class or the state.

There was something pathetic about al-Sadani's experiences in the Kuwaiti women's movement. Her 'ordinary' middle-class background, which was despised by the educated merchant-class women and which enabled her to focus on the question of gender and raise women's issues in a society divided between *asil* (noble origin) and *baisari* (non-noble), condemned her leadership of the feminist movement to failure. But though the merchant-class women despised her for being less educated and for coming from a different class, they still admired her courage in defying the patriarchal system.

There is a great similarity between the feminist issues raised by the AWDS and Western bourgeois feminism ('old-style women's rights feminism'[51]). However, before condemning the AWDS feminist values as a pure reflection of 'middle-class values', one should recognize al-Sadani's merit in identifying women as a unified and separate entity for whom the struggle for 'being' had just begun. She united women and raised the issues of women's rights, disturbing what had long been taken as an immutable and divinely ordered fact of life: the unequal relationships between men and women. This was in itself radical in a society which rested upon the principle of gender inequality.

The concept of women had been absent from the WCSS vocabulary. In fact, as has been pointed out, they added the word 'women' to their society only when told to do so by the government. They formed a society for women because the rules of sex segregation compelled them to do so, and remained silent on feminist issues. The Girls Club, born as a result of increased hostility between the WCSS and the AWDS, deepened the rivalry between the women's societies and highlighted the failure of Kuwaiti women to unite in their struggle towards their shared aspirations as women.

4
Contemporary Women's Organizations: Activities and Membership

The 1980s witnessed an unprecedented growth in the Islamic movement. Most researchers see this Islamic 'revival' as the result of economic, political, cultural and psychological factors;[1] they explain it in terms of class differences and the failure of Arab regimes to solve regional problems, as well as the influence of Westernization and anomie. The revival of Islamic values and beliefs presented itself as 'an alternative to the nationalist and socialist agenda',[2] offering a return to cultural authenticity.

Very little account has been taken of the relationship between patriarchy and the Islamic revival. My analysis of the Islamic revival in Kuwait (Chapter 5) suggests that there is a strong relationship between the rise of the feminist movement in the 1970s and the subsequent growth of the Islamic movement. The latter developed as a reaction to the women's movement, seeking to restore the patriarchal order which women's demand for autonomy had threatened to disrupt.

As noted earlier, the government—in its attempt to suppress Arab nationalism—had encouraged the proliferation of Islamic beliefs. But it soon found itself confronting the Islamic challenge: it responded by adopting an Islamic stand. In the early 1980s two Islamic women's organizations were established: Bayader al-Salam and the Islamic Care Society. These brought to four the total number of women's organizations.

This chapter examines the origins and objectives of the new women's organizations and discusses their activities and recruitment policies. It also looks at the activities of the WCSS and the Girls Club and tries to determine whether their objectives were redefined in reponse to the changing political climate of the 1980s.

Bayader al-Salam

The move towards establishing Bayader al-Salam began in the late 1970s with the arrival of a Syrian woman in Kuwait. This young woman, who later came to be known as the *da'iya* (preacher), had studied Islamic law in Damascus. She was not married and was in her early thirties. Her arrival in Kuwait was carefully planned by a wealthy Kuwaiti merchant, Yusuf al-Rifaie, who was himself married to a Syrian woman. Al-Rifaie had long been an outspoken opponent of the women's rights campaign. In 1973, as a member of the National Assembly, he led the opposition to the Equal Rights Bill, arguing that the 'liberation' of women would destroy the Muslim community and that restrictions on polygamy would lead to spinsterhood and *zina* (sexual liberty and adultery). In his words, 'All that those [men] who call for the liberation of women want is to be able to mix freely with them. . . . The true liberation for women is one which endows them with honour, respect, modesty and chastity. That is what is required.'[3]

Al-Rifaie was a strong believer in spiritual education. In 1988, in an interview with *al-Qabas* newspaper, he said:

> Spiritual education is vital for children. What Islam means by a spiritual education is the purification of the soul [*tazkiyat al-nafs*]; that is, to free the soul from ugly attributes and embellish it with divine virtues. It is also meant to endow the child with the principles of faith [*iman*], educate him/her to distinguish Islamic law [Shari'a] so that he/she becomes bound by belief and worship and relates to it [Islamic law] as a method and discipline and he/she will not know anything but Islam as religion, the Quran as faith [*iman*] and the Messenger [*al-rasul*] as leader and model.[4]

The *da'iya* was presumably asked to set up a spiritual organization. When she first arrived, she began to conduct religious gatherings for women. She read verses of the Quran and discussed the importance of religion in everyday life. According to her listeners, she was an excellent and captivating speaker and soon gathered a group of devoted Kuwaiti women followers, many from well-established merchant families and related to one another. In 1981 they established the first religious organization for women, Bayader al-Salam; they took as their motto the words 'faith and work', represented symbolically by a white dove, soaring in a blue sky, holding in its beak a bunch of wheat. Bayader al-Salam literally means the 'threshing floor of peace'.

The organizational structure of Bayader is quite revealing. As noted earlier, all voluntary associations in Kuwait have by law to follow a well-defined model of organization. Each association must have a written constitution and a board of regularly elected directors. Participation in decision-making is limited to Kuwaiti nationals; expatriates cannot hold office. Because of these rules a board of directors, composed of Kuwaiti members, was formed at Bayader, and Mrs Adela al-Othman, the daughter of a wealthy merchant, was elected president. It would be misleading, however, to regard the board of directors as an important source of power. In practice, the board has little significance; it is merely a response to externally imposed legal requirements.

Bayader is a religious organization which bears a direct resemblance to a mystical Sufi order. Sufi orders obey a specific system of religious ranking at the head of which is a *sheikh* (spiritual leader) to whom all members must show respect and devotion. The *sheikh* is related by chains of grace (and sometimes blood) to the founder of the order; apart from the request for obedience and loyalty, the *sheikh* does not enjoy absolute control over the members. Sufi organizations are known to be brotherhood associations which place their primary emphasis on 'fellowship as the dominant value'.[5] All members are equal and their relationship to the *sheikh* is defined in terms of *murshid* (teacher)/*murid* or *salik* (student) relationship. The *sheikh* is a teacher who guides the *salik* along the *tariqa* (spiritual path)[6] to the realization of *tawhid* (union with God) and supervises their progress. A *salik* who has succeeded in his or her spiritual quest may get permission from the *sheikh* to teach others the spiritual path of the Sufi order to which he or she belongs.[7] This was the case with the *da'iya* who came to Kuwait to set up a Sufi organization.

When Bayader was founded, its leaders must have faced an organizational dilemma: on the one hand, the society was affiliated to a spiritual order; on the other hand, it had to adopt a formal hierarchical structure defined on the basis of nationality. The problem was how to combine the two structures without affecting the basic Sufi organization. In response, a board of directors was created to deal mainly with public duties, such as giving interviews to the press and meeting government officials. The board members were selected from among the 19 Kuwaiti founders, known as the *muassisin*. The founders are in direct contact with the spiritual leader, with whom they share the burden of administrative responsibilities and maintain order and discipline within the society. They receive their spiritual education directly from the *da'iya* who acts as the principal *murshida* and in return they teach what they have learned to the new recruits. The real authority is vested in the hands of the *da'iya*, the spiritual leader of Bayader to whom all members owe loyalty, obedience and respect.

There are three crucial aspects of the group's structure: discipline, companionship and uniform. The entire organization is regulated by an impeccable system of discipline. Because their headquarters was erected as a place of worship, members and visitors must adopt certain behavioural patterns in recognition of, and respect for, its sanctity. For example, when entering the building, visitors must remove their shoes and leave them at the doorway. Inside, everyone must speak quietly, preferably in a whisper, and refrain from moving around the premises. The building is designed to allow maximum scrutiny on the inside and minimum penetrability from the outside.

The relationships between members are also disciplined, regulated by formal and informal mechanisms of control and sanction. Members are expected to show respect, loyalty and obedience to their teachers. The *salik* (member) has to make herself so transparent that the *murshida* can 'look through her'. This state of transparency, of complete 'nakedness', constitutes the essence of the loyalty between the *salik* and her *murshida*. If the *salik* fails to remain loyal, or behaves in an 'indecent' manner, she is liable to sanctions. The severity of the sanctions depends on the nature of the offence. In one particular case, a disobedient member was removed from her own *jama'a* (group). Her isolation lasted several months, during which her colleagues were not allowed to speak to her.[8] Such a separation can be a very painful experience.

Companionship (*jama'a*) is the basis of Bayader. In the well-ordered house of worship, it takes the form of sisterhood with all its expressions of solidarity, mutual trust and emotional ties. It is common to see members holding hands, smiling and comforting one another. Every now and then, an excursion is organized to reinforce the spirit of companionship. In all Sufi orders, the development of strong relationships between members, based on love, trust and mutual understanding, is an essential part of the *tariqa*:

> Companionship . . . gives numerous opportunities for mutual encouragement in the devout life and the practice of the virtues—that is, humility, generosity and equanimity—which lift from the heart the burdens weighing on it and, at the same time, embellish it, because they are the reflection of the Divine Qualities and are, according to the honoured saying, 'the tongues which glorify the Lord'.[9]

At the same time, companionship brings harmony and order to the organization. The member feels part of a group and it is to the group that she owes the utmost loyalty. In critical periods, companionship operates as a safety valve: it allows the individual to feel less pressure and, in the face of external attacks, serves to prevent the disintegration of the order.

A uniform way of dressing is important in Bayader, as in all Sufi orders. The costume must be in harmony with the spiritual quest: immaculately clean and simple. All Bayader members wear a long loose dress, with long sleeves, and cover their hair with a white scarf tied firmly round the neck. Though the uniforms are similar, the colour varies according to rank: dark blue for the spiritual leader, light blue for the founders (*muassisin*) and grey for the ordinary members.

Bayader's membership and recruitment strategies reflect the fact that in most voluntary associations in Kuwait, recruitment has been an issue of perennial concern. It is often feared that an open-door policy might bring new elements into the association who in turn might seriously challenge the existing board of directors at the next election. Fear of losing control has often led their leaders to restrict membership to friends and relatives. Bayader has not had to face this problem because, as noted above, the internal organization follows a different structure. Members are recruited to receive a spiritual education and to learn the *tariqa*. The spread of the *tariqa* is important to all Sufi orders, as it ensures its continuity.

In the early days, Bayader's leaders mainly targeted young students and college graduates. A researcher who visited the society in the early 1980s noted that, 'The association consists mainly of recent college and post-secondary education graduates, who are working and/or housewives, college students, and secondary school students.'[10] Most Bayader leaders work as teachers in government schools where they seek to strengthen their contacts with students. Those students who show an interest in religious matters are invited to attend the group's religious gatherings. The leaders also seek to bring their relatives and friends into the society and they visit mosques to seek potential members.

Recruits must undergo a strict test of faith before being admitted as full members. Bayader leaders are very cautious. New recruits are organized into small groups and placed under the guidance of a *murshida*, from whom they receive general religious instruction. For months thereafter, they are tested on their religious knowledge and their daily prayers, and are observed in their interactions within the group. Only those who pass the examinations are recruited as members. Those who fail are discouraged from seeking entry to the group, and are advised to attend the *muntadas* (religious gatherings) which are held weekly at the society and are open to non-members.

Within less than a year of its establishment, Bayader's membership had reached 100 and the *muntadas* were attracting hundreds of women. In the early 1980s there was a genuine enthusiasm for Bayader among young Kuwaiti women. Almost all the schoolgirls interviewed during this period mentioned that their time was divided between school and Bayader.[11] The group's immediate popularity did not stem from the fact that it was the first religious group for women. It was the way Bayader was organized that appealed to young women: the emphasis placed upon companionship, the serenity of its leaders and their smiling faces. Furthermore, Islam is presented as a harmonious and genuine religion which, when embraced fully, brings both joy and tranquillity. The emphasis is put on the self rather than politics, on spiritual realization rather than material success. For many who feel either alienated or disenchanted with Western values, the teachings of Bayader give new meaning to their lives. According to one member:

> Islam brings one happiness. It gives guidance. I was not veiled before, I had studied in Egypt. Yet I felt lost. Every day, I did the same thing, I put on different clothes, it was meaningless. I did not find happiness. I got married, I had children and it was all the same. One day, when I came to Bayader to listen to their seminars, I saw one of the members. Her face was full of light, untroubled and peaceful. I said to myself, if being a member of Bayader would make me like her, why shouldn't I become a member? So I did.

Were it not for persistent attacks by orthodox religious circles and secular groups, Bayader's leaders would have tripled or even quadrupled the membership in less than four years, but by 1988 the organization had only 200 members. The attacks led the leaders to become more vigilant, making inquiries about every woman who came to the society. The comings and goings of visitors were carefully recorded and they were all asked to leave their names, phone numbers and addresses in a registry book at the reception desk. Those considered to bc a potential threat were prevented from returning to the society.

The attacks, which began in the early 1980s, were launched by the Ikhwan (Muslim Brotherhood) and some Salafi (traditional/ancestral) groups who feared for their own popularity. These two Islamic groups depended heavily on women to spread their beliefs and maintain their existence. In 1983 the Ikhwan responded to the creation of Bayader by establishing a women's committee at their headquarters. The Salafi group issued a series of books and articles condemning Sufism as un-Islamic.[12]

Persistently attacked by more orthodox religious circles and continually defending themselves by denying their affiliation to a Sufi order, Bayader leaders then found themselves under attack from a different direction. This time, it was a secular group composed of five women who were not affiliated to any particular women's organization or engaged in the feminist movement. They were strong supporters of the Tali'a group (the Arab nationalists) and were anxious to stop the spread of Islam. In 1984 these young women took the *da'iya* to court for holding a public gathering at a government establishment without official authorization and during working hours. After a trial lasting several days, the *da'iya* was fined the small sum of KD40. In spite of the ordeal of the trial, news of which filled the newspapers for days, as well as the persistent attacks from religious groups, Bayader has survived. Although it has fewer members, there is a strong and indivisible solidarity between them.

A primary activity for Bayader is the teaching of Islam. The organization has developed into a kind of mystical school which provides women and children with numerous year-round *muntadas*, courses in *tajwid* (reading the Quran) and lessons in *sirat al-nabi* (the life of the Prophet). In addition, children are taught *anashid* (mystical songs) and entertained with puppet shows. For Bayader's leaders, children are 'the seeds of today and the trees of tomorrow'. For this reason, greater emphasis is placed on the religious education of young children; during the long summer months, special religious programmes are organized for them. All the teaching is carried out by the spiritual leader and the *muassisin*.

Members help the leaders organize the educational programmes for children, and many of them also act as supervisors. They attend lessons and take part in religious gatherings. But, unlike non-members, young recruits are active listeners who have given the oath to their *murshida* and have begun their journey along the spiritual path. Organized in small groups directly under the guidance of a *murshida*, all members are constantly assessed, questioned and observed in their daily activities.

The love of God lies at the heart of Bayader's teachings. God is unique (*la illah ila allah*) and it is to Him, the One without equal, that the heart needs to turn:

> The heart is perpetually longing for the Lord; it is a pure and true feeling that nothing in the being could fill the emptiness except the perfect link with the Lord of Being (*rab al-wujud*). The more a human being worships God faithfully and sincerely and is truthful in his inclinations, places himself within His hands and supplicates . . . the more he will find his lost soul . . . find the Supreme Being . . . and discover Spiritual Joy

> . . . represented in what the Generous Messenger (*al-rasul al-karim*) has called the 'sweetness of paradise'. . . . The heart will not thrive, nor be good, nor prosperous, nor joyful, nor delighted, nor restful, nor serene except when loving his God.[13]

The Perfect Love leads one to *ma'rifa* (the knowledge of God) and ultimately to the realization of *tawhid* (union) with the Divine Being. But, first, to love God is to make God the only object of worship. This worship is to be manifested through the true practice of Islamic rites (i.e. daily prayers, fasting, *zakat* [religious tax destined for the poor] and the *hajj* [pilgrimage]), supplications and sessions of *dhikr* (the invocation of God's name):

> Worship leads to those majestic and beautiful qualities in the human soul [*nafs*] and gives the religion its soul, its life and beauty, and from it emanates a true [spiritual] state convinced of God's existence, contemplating God and aspiring to obey Him; and a feeling bursts out, controls the heart, and rests in its existence and being. . . . Worship has different colours, some of which are: prayers, *zakat*, fasting, pilgrimage, the Quran, *dhikr* and *du'a* [invocation].[14]

Acts of worship occupy a central place in Bayader's teachings. They are obligatory exercises for every woman who has devoted herself to becoming a member and a *salik* (spiritual seeker). Each member is asked to note carefully and honestly on her *jadwal al-ibada* (worship chart) the number of *salat* (obligatory prayers) and *nawafil* (additional prayers) she performs daily, the number of times she asks for *istighfar* (God's forgiveness) and the length of time she devotes to reading the Quran and studying Islam (see Table 1, p. 112). Based on this, the *murshida* assesses a member's commitment and faith. Members are also expected to participate in the collective performances of remembrance (i.e. *dhikr* sessions) during which certain Quranic verses are recited rhythmically. The *dhikr* sessions are a central ritual in all Sufi orders; though they vary from one order to another, they are basically intended to create a mystical state. Hence, whether alone or in the company of others, the *salik* is put in a continuous state of remembrance of God's existence.

The worship exercises (prayers and *dhikr*) are not an end in themselves, but are simply a means by which to establish contact with God. In Sufism, Islamic rites (prayers, pilgrimage, *zakat* and fasting) are seen as important methods of *tazkiyat al-nafs* (self-purification). For instance, during the lunar month of Ramadan, when Muslims fast from dawn to sunset, a believer must abstain from eating, drinking and sexual relations. Fasting is said to be a method of self-discipline and self-detachment from worldly concerns and sexual desire, which trains the *nafs* (self)[15] to acquire the divine virtues of abstinence, renunciation and patience. Sexual desire, material possessions, greed and jealousy are all conceived of as worldly concerns which imprison the soul and distract the heart from loving God.

Bayader's leaders put a strong emphasis on *tazkiyat al-nafs*, for self-purification and detachment draw the seeker closer to God the Beloved. Broadly speaking, self-purification is not so much the negation of one's worldly desires as the transcendence of those desires for the love of God. In other words, it is 'the transformation of desire from self-centredness to God-centredness'.[16]

Several women who have devoted themselves to the spiritual path have opted for *uzuba* (celibacy); one example is the famous Sufi saint Rabi'a al-Adawiya of Basra who devoted her life entirely to God. But, however ideal it might be for those who want to lead a mystical life, Sufis have never praised celibacy highly. This is because Islam has sanctified the union between man and woman and made marriage the duty of all Muslims. The Prophet is reported to have said, 'If a person marries, he has fulfilled half the religion.'[17]

In recent years, Bayader has begun to look for ways to reach illiterate and deprived women. In 1987 it established the Zakat Committee for Charity and Blessing. Islam orders that all dutiful Muslims, particularly the well-off, must give *zakat*. The committee collects the *zakat* from those who are willing to pay it and then distributes it to poor families. But the committee's intentions are not simply to provide charity for the poor; they also aim 'to raise their Islamic consciousness', that is, 'to guide them towards hygiene, thrift and tidiness, and towards adherence to Islam by following the deeds of the Prophet and his teachings'.[18]

The Islamic Care Society

The Islamic Care Society (al-Ri'aya al-Islamiya) was founded in 1982 and was given the AWDS headquarters which had taken the AWDS leaders almost seven years to build, marking the end of an era which had seen women's organizations calling for equal rights. The woman behind the foundation of the society was Sheikha Latifa Fahed al-Salem Al Sabah, the wife of the Crown Prince and Prime Minister. Since the mid-1970s Sheikha Latifa had been trying to draw women's attention to Islam. In 1976 the

Fatima mosque was built in Abdullah al-Salem, one of the richest suburbs of Kuwait city. Sheikha Latifa visited the mosque, befriended a group of women who came regularly to pray, and suggested organizing lectures and religious seminars for women at the mosque.[19] Her initiative coincided with the period when the government was trying to curtail the influence of the nationalist groups and when Kuwaiti women were calling for equal rights. This group of Kuwaiti women, some of whom came from well-established merchant families, welcomed Sheikha Latifa's proposition. Religious lectures and discussions were soon held in the mosque under the supervision of Sheikh Hassan Tannoon.[20]

As attendance increased, a library was installed at the request of Sheikha Latifa and lectures were given three times a week. At that time (1977) the idea arose of setting up a centre for Quranic teaching (Dar al-Quran) for women instead of lessons in the mosque. Umm Attiya al-Ansaria, a girls' school, was chosen as a location. Two factors guided this choice: first, the school was situated near the Fatima mosque; and, second, the school's headmistress, Mrs Dalal al-Bisher, was well known to Sheikha Latifa since they had worked together in organizing the religious seminars at the mosque. Mrs al-Bisher was appointed supervisor of Dar al-Quran. Sheikha Latifa donated vast sums of money to the centre. The Ministry of Awqaf [Religious Endowments] and Islamic Affairs also gave financial support on a monthly basis.[21] The centre expanded rapidly and by 1984 the number of female students amounted to 2,680, far exceeding the total number of male students, which was reported to be 949.[22]

One might ask why Sheikha Latifa was interested in setting up a religious society for women when Dar al-Quran was successfully reaching its target audience. The answer lies in the growing strength of the Ikhwan and the popularity of Bayader al-Salam, which took the government by surprise. It was not the presence of such organizations that was of particular concern to the government, but rather the lack of an alternative religious society. This lack seemed dangerous because more women might choose to join Bayader or the Ikhwan. As a religious school, Dar al-Quran did not carry the same weight as a *da'wa* (mission) society, such as Bayader or the Social Reform Society. Moreover, the teachings of Bayader and the Ikhwan, with their emphasis on loyalty and obedience to God alone, threatened the very basis of a secular national identity. For this reason, the government saw its task not simply as supporting the Islamization programmes but, more important, as reinforcing the spirit of patriotism within an Islamic framework.

In 1982 Sheikha Latifa called upon the same group of women who had helped her organize the religious seminars at the mosque. These women, now in their late forties, were as enthusiastic as before about working with

Sheikha Latifa. Together, they established the Islamic Care Society (ICS). Its objectives were to 'purify' Islam from distorted interpretations, to 'propagate' the true Islam and to 'build a Muslim life' in which the individual is a 'member of a family and the society':

First, calling people towards Islam by:
1. preaching and explaining the elements of Islam;
2. constantly persuading [people] by various educational and cultural means to build a Muslim life based on the correct Islamic values in which the individual is a member of a family and the society; and
3. building schools, dispensaries, hospitals and other charitable institutions to look after deserving people in a very Islamic atmosphere which will also make Islam more appealing.

Second, religious goals achieved by:
1. purifying Islamic thoughts; and
2. giving consideration to the teaching of the Quran and *sunnah* [the Prophet Muhammad's words and deeds].

Third, cultural objectives which include:
1. the propagation of modern cultural behaviour within the framework of Islam;
2. the revival of the Islamic heritage and the attempt to co-ordinate it with modern science and future aspirations; and
3. the bestowing of scholarships on deserving candidates.

Fourth, social aims as follows:
1. possible help for individuals and families in the Islamic world; and
2. co-operation with Islamic establishments and societies worldwide.

Fifth, the propagation of Islamic teachings and values through various media, i.e. seminars, conferences, lectures, books and magazines.[23]

The organizational structure of the ICS is like that of all the voluntary associations in Kuwait. It has adopted a centralized bureaucratic structure with Sheikha Latifa as honorary chairwoman and Mrs al-Bisher as president. The society has eight officers and two categories of members: ordinary and *muntasibin* (affiliated). The latter category includes all non-Kuwaiti members and those under 18 years of age who are not entitled to vote or run for office, but who take part in the society's activities. The society also has a number of paid workers: two secretaries, a driver, a male porter, and a maid in charge of preparing tea and coffee. In addition, Sheikha Latifa has her own (male) secretary who comes to the society's office every other day to collect the mail and communicate the Sheikha's instructions.

Though she holds the title of honorary chairwoman, Sheikha Latifa takes an active part in running the society. She is also involved in the selection of leaders. When I asked an official how she became a board member, her answer was:

> When I went to see the Crown Prince and Prime Minister to present him with my recent publication on Islam, he introduced me to his wife. We met and she asked me to become a member of the ICS. I was asked to stand in the elections to become a board member. Later, Sheikha Latifa asked me to be the head of the Cultural Committee.

The official further pointed out that 'all decisions concerning the society are taken at the top'.

Once a year, members are entitled to give their views on matters relating to the society's activities. This takes place during the general assembly when final reports are read and financial accounts approved. Every four years, members are called to elect their representatives. Constitutionally, it is permissible for office holders to be re-elected to the same positions for an indefinite period of time. So far, there have been no changes within the managing board since the establishment of the ICS. For the last two general elections, officials have been re-elected to the same positions.

Unlike Bayader, the ICS does not impose any kind of discipline upon its members. They can laugh, talk loudly and drink tea in the common room. They do not need to remove their shoes or wear Islamic dress. The ambiance is quite mixed: a woman in contemporary veiled dress, one in Western-style clothes and one in the traditional Kuwaiti *abbaya* can all be seen mingling together.

There is a significant difference, in both content and form, between the traditional *abbaya* and *zayy al-islami* (Islamic dress). The *abbaya* is a black cloak which Kuwaiti women wear to cover themselves in public; it is regarded as a symbol of female seclusion. Islamic dress, on the other hand, consists of a *hijab* (headcover) and a loose garment intended to hide the body except for the face and hands. It made its appearence with the recent Islamic 'revival' and is meant to convey an aura of respect and dignity: 'it tells the public, particularly the male public, that although a woman has left the house to study and work, she is respectable and does not expect to be harassed'.[24]

The recruitment strategies of the ICS reflect the leaders' need to maintain control over the society by remaining in office. Any distribution of power would affect the society's policies. Sheikha Latifa knew from the very beginning that, in order to achieve the society's objectives, she needed to rely on loyal friends and to keep a good grip on the organization.

But the constitution raises a problem: members must elect their representatives. When, in 1962, the government introduced the concept of an elected board, it was expected to bring order and democracy to the voluntary associations: members would elect their representatives, who in turn would work to serve the interests of the association and its members. What the government failed to realize was that once members are elected to office, they are unlikely to give up their leadership positions and return to anonymity unless forced to do so.[25] More important, the leaders need to remain in office in order to carry out the goals of the organizations which they themselves have established.

In order to secure their re-election, office-holders often recruit their own friends and kin whom they refer to as *rab'*, forming a cohesive social network within the society. The *rab'* are an important social category that can be found in every women's organization. The concept of *rab'* means more than just being friends and kin. A woman who left the Girls Club to join the ICS said, 'My *rab'* who were with me at the Girls Club have also changed to the ICS. We are a complete group. We are six women. We are the kind who support each other and work together.' The *rab'* stay together constantly and enjoy being in each other's company. They often join the same organization and do things together, such as shopping, making pilgrimages and paying social visits. They are intimate friends who support one another emotionally and even financially.

To the leaders, the *rab'* become a group of faithful supporters whom they trust and can count upon when they need their help in the elections. It is important for office holders to have their *rab'* in the society. Most of the women whom I interviewed about their motives for joining the ICS said that they had been invited by the president, who happened to be either one of their friends, or a relative, or someone they had met at a social event. Only about one third of the members joined the society because they 'want to make friends and kill time', as one member put it.

As a result, the ICS has come to be composed mostly of middle-aged and elderly women, similar in age to the leaders. The predominance of this age group has had the effect of driving younger women away and attracting older members. The latter have all said that they are much happier to be in the company of women of a similar age. One member told me, 'Here [at the ICS], you can relate to and interact more easily with members because they are all the same age as you are. It is because of this that I feel more relaxed here and feel as if I am part of them.' Although most of the members belong to the same age group, they are not all housewives. It is only because housewives tend to come to the society more often than other members that the ICS has come to be known as the Housewives Society (Jam'iyat Sayyidat al-Buyut).[26]

Not all the members are drawn from the dominant classes (i.e. the ruling family and the merchant class). Many come from the well-established Kuwaiti families who traditionally represented the *nukhoda* class. These women tend to describe themselves as being *wasat* (in the middle) and *busata'* (simple). 'Here', explained a member, 'we are all of the same rank and, unlike the other women's organizations, our society is open to anyone and all the members are *busata*". Members also like to think of themselves as being *wasat*, that is, 'in between', neither too snobbish or liberal (like the Girls Club and the WCSS) nor too strict (like Bayader al-Salam). Such a strong ideological demarcation between 'us' and 'them' is peculiar not only to the ICS. Almost all the women's societies tend to build upon this dichotomy of us and them, partly to reinforce group identification and partly to facilitate the exclusion of other social groups.

The ICS is engaged in a number of activities. Direct collaboration with the Ministry of Awqaf and Islamic Affairs was central to the foundation of the society. From the moment that Dar al-Quran was established, Sheikha Latifa formed an Advisory Committee composed of five male religious scholars. This committee provides the ICS with information on religious matters and issues the books and pamphlets which are intended to 'propagate the correct Islamic values'. So far, the ICS has published a series of books on *hajj* (pilgrimage) and *sawm* (fasting), and on Islam in general. Emphasis is placed on the outward aspects of Islam such as the observance of Islamic rites (prayers, pilgrimage and fasting) and the doing of *ihsan* (good deeds). According to the president of the society:

> Islam is lenient; it is not harsh or difficult. In Kuwait, many people are harsh in their interpretation of Islam, but Islam is about the treatment of others and kindness. The distinctive trait of our organization is that it has both veiled and unveiled women. We believe in the true *iman* [faith] and not in blind worship and the veil.

To the ICS leaders, the 'truc Islam' is demonstrated in the doing of good deeds and the 'caring for others'. Care means 'mercy, charity, kindness and feeling for others'.[27] According to Sheikha Latifa, 'this in reality is what Allah has bequeathed us to believe in'.[28] The whole essence of Islam is said to be fraternity, loyalty to the country and good works. It is this kind of Islam that the ICS leaders want to disseminate:

> We call upon you, our Muslim brothers and sisters, to adhere to the precepts of our true religion and to love deeply the members of the Muslim community. . . . With all our faith, we set out to *serve this*

> *country*, which gives so much and requests a great deal. Let's be more positive in our understanding of this *watan* [homeland], which requests from us that we give with utmost loyalty.[29] [Emphasis added]

ICS leaders constantly call on both men and women to love and serve their *watan*. Expressions such as *baladi al-aziz* (our dearest homeland), *watani al-habib* (our beloved country), *li maslahat al-watan* (for the interests of the country), *iklas lil-watan* (loyalty to the country), and *khidmat al-watan* (serving the country) appear frequently in their speeches and publications.

In 1986 Kuwait became the headquarters of the International Islamic Charitable Foundation, for which the government gave support and provided funds. In December 1987 the ICS launched a one-week campaign to raise funds for the foundation. The slogan was, 'Pay a dinar and save a Muslim.' In less than two days, the leaders raised KD7,000. As one official reported, 'Members of the Foundation were very pleased with us.'

The leaders also seek to 'revive' the traditional role of women and to promote the model of a woman who is pious but not fanatic, who appreciates modern life but is not too Westernized. To these ends, the society offers classes for women in embroidery, dressmaking, oriental cookery and *tawjid* (reading the Quran). Classes are not free: fees range between KD10 and KD25, depending on the course. In 1989 the leaders introduced a course in English conversation. One of the officials explained:

> It is useful for women to learn how to speak English. All households have maids who speak English and we want to teach housewives how to communicate with their maids. The other point is that most women travel abroad. We want to teach them how to ask for things in shops and how to order food in restaurants, and so on.

The most popular class is dressmaking. The 1980s saw a growing interest in the subject, particularly among expatriate women, partly because it is seen as part of the role of the good Muslim housewife to know how to sew, and partly because of the government's 'Kuwaitization' policy in the labour market which had the effect of reducing the job opportunities available to expatriates. There was also a growing demand for female dressmakers as a result of the Islamic revival and the appearance of Islamic dress. Until fairly recently, almost all the dressmakers in Kuwait were men who had come from India in the early 1950s and had monopolized the trade for almost three decades. Of the 109 women I interviewed about their reasons for taking dressmaking classes, 60 said that they wanted to become dressmakers.

Dressmaking classes are an important source of revenue for the ICS, bringing in KD15,715 in 1987 alone. In addition to providing dressmaking and cookery classes, the society runs public seminars. In 1986 the leaders held a series of seminars on the duties of Muslim mothers.

The ICS also operates as a social club. The leaders have adopted the male concept of *diwaniya*: at their informal gatherings every Tuesday, at least 20 women come regularly to drink tea and talk about various issues. According to one member, 'We talk about cooking, children, treatment by husbands and about the maids. Everyone speaks. It's the kind of gathering where one gives vent to one's inner feelings. Every woman gives her opinions and advises others if needed.' The *diwaniya* provides an opportunity for those who have been busy with their immediate families to catch up with the latest gossip in town, and for the few lonely widows there is a chance to meet other women and pass the time pleasantly. ICS members also get together on national holidays. Occasionally, they visit the children at the orphanage. The president said, 'We want to attract them to the *mujtama'* (community) and make them feel part of it.'

Unlike the WCSS, the ICS plays only a marginal role in international conferences. In 1985 two ICS officials went to Nairobi to attend the UN World Conference on Women. Apart from this unique occasion, the society has had very little contact with international women's organizations. On the regional level, however, it plays a more active role. The leaders take part in regional conferences and make official visits to Saudi Arabia and other neighbouring Gulf states.

The Women's Cultural and Social Society

The large, two-storey administrative building that took WCSS leaders 10 years to build now stands majestically in the quiet suburb of Khaldiya. The ground-floor entrance opens onto a spacious hall which functions mainly as a waiting room. To the far left of the hall a big door leads to the offices of the secretaries and the president. Board members do not have their own offices: they either work in the meeting room next to the president's office or use the secretary's desk. The upper floor is rarely used and seems deserted all year round. It contains two large rooms which are occasionally used for general meetings, conferences or social gatherings.

The building seems a semi-deserted palace. Since the mid-1980s participation in the society has declined significantly and members only come occasionally to the headquarters. Most of the work is done by the president, the officers and the secretaries. In the early 1980s the president, Lulua al-

Qitami, was exempted by the government from her duties as head of the girls' college to become a full-time salaried official of the WCSS.

Over the last 25 years, there have been very few changes in the membership composition. The society has retained its exclusive character, drawing its members from the most prominent merchant-class families. Between 1972 and 1987 the number of members rose from 32 to 92. Professional women from well-to-do families joined the society and as the daughters and cousins of the founders grew old enough, they came to join their kin. Mothers, daughters, aunts and cousins are all members. More than two-thirds of WCSS members are related. While the older generation are either housewives or run their own businesses, the younger members work in the most prestigious and high-ranking jobs in Kuwait. Many are managers, school headmistresses, or government advisers in the fields of health and education.

There has been little rivalry over the leadership positions. Most members are pleased to delegate responsibilities to those few who are interested in holding office. It is at the leadership level that problems have emerged. The president had a tendency to control all the activities, delegating few responsibilities to members and officers. In 1988 she did not, for instance, authorize the treasurer to issue cheques without her consent.

The president's autocratic attitude irritated two young professionals who, when the situation became intolerable, resigned as board members. The existence of a strong kin network allowed the president (whose mother, sister and cousins are all in the society, some of them holding office) to maintain her position. One member commented, 'The election is achieved by means of the sister and cousin relations. The board of directors elects the president. The board is elected by the members. During the last election, there were 50 women voting, all related.'

For 20 years, Lulua al-Qitami had been president of the WCSS and was regarded by her kin network as indispensable to the society. A leader's principal source of power is found in his or her indispensability[30]—this quality made al-Qitami's re-election a pure formality and no one contested her leadership. It was not until January 1993 that al-Qitami resigned and Mrs Adela al-Sayer, a board member, was elected president of the WCSS.

In general, the president is in charge of all official duties, such as representing Kuwaiti women abroad and dealing with the state administration. Each group of officers is in charge of a particular committee. By the late 1980s there were four committees: the Zakat Committee, the Adult Literacy Committee, the Cancer Committee and the Social Committee. Three secretaries are in charge of all the administrative work. The following extract from my field notes is an example of a typical working day:

> I arrived at 9.45 this morning. The secretaries were already there, moving around and complaining about too much work. Preparations for tomorrow's meeting were well underway. 4.30 pm: Awatef is still typing. Madiha has finished arranging the files in the office; she is now calling an agency to order new envelopes for the society. Afaf is phoning the members to ask them to bring food for Tuesday night's dinner party. 5.00 pm: Afaf has just finished calling the members; she is now contacting the press to inform them about tomorrow's meeting. The president has requested that they have reporters in the morning to take a few photos of the meeting. Afaf, with the help of Awatef, has selected a number of female reporters with whom the society has good relationships. 5.30 pm: Awatef has finished typing. She has gone to check the conference room and set up the projector in case the president wants to show the visitors slides of Hanan village, and Afaf is making sure that the microphones are ready for tomorrow.

At Bayader al-Salam, there is no such distinction between secretary and members. The administrative work is done by the members. At the ICS, the two secretaries are mainly in charge of answering outside calls and typing.

The activities of the WCSS can be divided into official duties, social welfare, and educational and social programmes. Speaking of official duties, al-Qitami explained that 'our society is semi-governmental; that is, we follow and execute state policies and represent the country at international conferences'. She added, 'When I go to attend any international conference, I go as a government representative.' As noted earlier, in the mid-1970s with the declaration of the UN Decade for Women, the government recognized the WCSS as an official organization whose leader was to speak officially on behalf of Kuwaiti women. Participation in international women's conferences has become one of the main priorities of the WCSS.

Lulua al-Qitami played an active role in international conferences. She attended the UN Conferences on Women in Mexico City (1975), Copenhagen (1980) and Nairobi (1985), and also all the Pan-Arab Conferences on Women, consistently presenting Kuwait as a 'modern', 'democratic' country where women participate 'side by side' with men in national development, 'thanks to the unlimited aid and encouragement of the government'.[31] All foreign delegates who come to Kuwait on official visits are taken to the WCSS to meet the president. Her duty is to inform them about 'Kuwaiti women's achievements' and to provide them with leaflets and coloured brochures on women's organizations in Kuwait.

It was the change in the status of the WCSS, from a voluntary association to a semi-governmental organization, which led al-Qitami to set up an official bureaucratic structure for the Regional Conferences on Women. In March 1984 a statutory body in the form of a Supreme Committee was created to supervise the regional conferences. The committee was called the Women's Co-ordinating Committee for the Gulf and the Arabian Peninsula; the WCSS president was elected secretary-general. Its stated purpose is 'to work towards co-ordinating the activities and endeavours of women in the Gulf in order to help them participate in the social, cultural and economic transformation, with the aim of serving the process of development in the region'.[32]

Social welfare is central to the WCSS: of all the women's societies, it has been the most involved in charity work. 'For us,' explained a member, 'the giving of charity is something hereditary.' 'We like to donate,' said another; 'it is within us, we do it with great joy—to the extent that we allow our maids to live with us, we clothe them and take them around with us.' Apart from being seen as something 'hereditary', charity is conceived of as a moral and social duty. In the words of members, 'If the individual is well off, shouldn't he or she help others? Anyone who reads the Quran would realize that it is our duty to help the poor.' Women are regarded as 'better' than men at charity work. One argued, 'It is a natural thing for a woman to do because she has a maternal instinct.'

In 1978 the WCSS embarked on a large-scale charitable project in Sudan. It consisted of building an entire village in the Kassala region, some 1,000 kilometres from the capital, Khartoum. Hanan village includes, among many other facilities, schools for boys and girls, a kindergarten, a women's training centre, a technical training centre for boys, dormitories, a mosque and a medical centre. Designed in close collaboration with the Sudanese Ministry of Awqaf and Islamic Affairs, the village was intended to be self-sufficient, accommodating orphans who were victims of the war. In the village, boys would be trained to do 'masculine' jobs and girls would be taught sewing and other types of 'women's work'. As one officer explained, 'Girls will be supervised all the time and they will not leave the village before they get married because otherwise they will be in danger and it is *haram* (shameful) to educate them and then leave them. But boys can leave and work outside the village.'

To raise funds for the village, the WCSS leaders developed the concept of *tabaq al-khair* (the bowl of charity) as an important religious and charitable event. *Tabaq al-khair* is held on the day of *mawlad al-nabi* (the birth of the Prophet) and consists of selling a variety of foods prepared by women and children. Ten such charity fairs have been held so far and the society raised KD2 million for Hanan village which was completed in 1988.

Apart from this grandiose project, for which al-Qitami was awarded the title 'Humanitarian Woman of the Year 1987', in 1981 the society established a Zakat Committee, the first in Kuwait. By 1988 the committee was providing financial assistance to 73 orphans and 437 poor families, of which 77 were Kuwaiti.

In addition to providing charity, the WCSS seeks to comfort the sick. In 1983 the society established the Cancer Committee to provide moral support for cancer patients. The committee has six members who regularly visit the hospital, give gifts to the patients and entertain them. To provide financial help for the patients, many of whom come from very poor families, the committee organizes annual charity bazaars.

In terms of educational and social programmes, the society runs literacy classes for adult women. These were introduced in 1987 in collaboration with the Ministry of Education and were free of charge. In October 1987, 57 illiterate women enrolled. They were given lessons in Arabic, maths and reading the Quran. During the same year, the WCSS ran a series of seminars designed to 'benefit women' and to help them understand their role in the family better. The seminar topics included: how to look after your health; how to serve your husband; how to be a good housewife; and how to behave with your 20-year-old daughter and prepare her for married life. In 1988 the society started cookery classes. The fee for the three-month course was KD30. Unlike the ICS courses, the WCSS classes offered international cuisine in collaboration with the wives of diplomats and some renowned hotel chefs.

The WCSS continues to held tea parties for the wives of diplomats and for visiting officials. As noted in the previous chapter, the WCSS has always felt it important 'to consolidate relationships between the wives of diplomats and the ladies of Kuwait'.[33] But members no longer organize frequent social parties within the society. Since the 1970s merchant-class women have embarked on a new lifestyle and tend to host lavish dinner parties at home.

The Girls Club

As noted earlier, the Girls Club was born in 1975 as a result of increased rivalry between the WCSS and the AWDS. Founded by a group of related merchant-class women, the club was not officially open to the public until April 1980 when the opening ceremony was attended by members of the ruling family and several important government officials.

The club leaders were soon to be confronted with the obstacles of government bureaucracy and faced vigorous opposition to their establishment. The opposition was launched, in the early 1980s, by the conservative male members of the Municipal Council who did not approve of a women's sports club. Nor could they tolerate the club's 'liberalism' which they feared might have a 'bad influence' on women. In 1985, in a letter addressed to the Ministry of Social Affairs and Labour, the Municipal Council announced its decision to demolish the club and to use the 10,000 square metres of land as a public park. The club leaders then used their kin relations to put pressure on the Municipal Council. The Council of Ministers intervened, requesting that the council review its decision. A year later, however, in April 1986, the Municipal Council reaffirmed its intention to demolish the club. At that time, faced with growing opposition, the government dissolved both the National Assembly and the Municipal Council. For the Girls Club, however, the problem was far from over.

Without going into details about land regulations, suffice it to say that the Girls Club had the misfortune to occupy a piece of land which was not registered under the ministry's Property Act. This is because in the mid-1970s, when the club was licensed, the Ministry of Social Affairs and Labour was short of premises. The club's leaders wanted a piece of land large enough to build all kinds of sports facilities. At that time, the municipality agreed temporarily to provide the Girls Club with 10,000 square metres of land. Soon afterwards, the club leaders built two tennis courts, a basketball court, a swimming pool, an indoor gymnasium and a one-storey administrative building.

The uncertainty about the future of the club led the leaders to rethink their policies. 'Our problem', explained an official, 'is to get the club taken care of. The government did not give us the right to use the land. We want to establish our identity.' By establishing their 'identity', they meant increasing club membership and forcing the government to recognize the importance of the club for women.

The internal organization of the Girls Club is similar to that of the WCSS and the ICS. It is highly bureaucratic and hierarchical, and the board has total control over the club. All decisions taken by the board are later communicated to the members. A *diwaniya*-type meeting is held every Tuesday to allow members to voice their concerns and suggest new ideas. So far, members' attendance at the *diwaniya* has been minimal. The number rarely exceeds 25 out of 1,467 club members—a mere 2 per cent of the membership.

The club also has a number of paid workers: three secretaries, two servants (an Indian married couple), a gate-keeper and five physical trainers. Members are divided into two categories: ordinary and *muntasibin* (affiliated). The former are Kuwaitis over 18 years old who hold the right to elect their representatives and to run for office. Although constitutionally all ordinary members have equal rights to hold office, in practice such rights have been tactfully circumscribed. For the last 15 years, the leadership of the club has been confined to its founders, the *muassisin*.

In 1987, as a result of uncertainty about the club's future and the leaders' inability to reach a consensus on the strategies needed to win control over the club, the board faced a redistribution of power among its officers. The president, who was accused of being autocratic and inefficient, lost her leadership position in the election. She was, however, retained as a board member. Sheikha Sabiha Al Sabah, a member of the ruling family, became the new president. But apart from a redistribution of power, the club has kept its initial officers. The *rab'* strategy made it possible for the officers to demote the leader without creating many schisms or conflicts within the board. In asking their friends and relatives to vote for Sheikha Sabiha, the officers played on the need to save the club from being demolished.

Like most women's organizations, the leaders have their own *rab'* acting as a support group to keep the club from falling into the hands of outsiders. This explains why, since 1975, the leaders have been able to retain their control over the club in spite of an increase in membership. The *rab'* do not necessarily take part in the club's activities. One young member told me, 'My mother has been registered as a member ever since the club was founded but she's never come to the club and doesn't even know where it's located.' It is often during the elections that the *rab'* make their appearance.

The club has the largest membership of all the women's societies in Kuwait—in 1987 it counted 1,467 members. In particular, the availability of sports facilities has attracted women to the club. There is no shortage of private health clubs and sports facilities in Kuwait, but health clubs tend to cater for the wealthy and charge exorbitant fees, ranging from KD60 to KD100 for a period of three months, whereas the Girls Club annual membership fee only amounts to KD25. The club also has the advantage of being exclusively for women and of providing sports facilities in a simple and informal atmosphere.

The club offers a range of sports facilities (tennis, swimming and basketball) and provides classes in aerobics, a popular activity, offered twice a day in the gymnasium. The club leaders occasionally organize tennis and basketball tournaments between their own team and the female teams of other clubs and societies. For the first time, in 1986, the club's gymnastic team travelled abroad to compete in Tunisia. The club also holds frequent public debates on various topical issues related to women and the family. In 1989 classes in English and French were introduced.

Conclusion

In almost all the women's organizations in Kuwait, the *rab'* emerge as an important source of control and a strategy for perpetuating power. In order to retain their influence and avoid a redistribution of power, the leaders bring their own friends and relatives into the society. But whereas this strategy has enabled the leaders to secure their positions and maintain their hold over their particular organizations, it has made it impossible for other women to be involved in decision-making. Leadership positions have remained the privilege of a few, and it is these very few who have gained popularity and prestige. Leaders meet with government officials, give interviews to the press and travel all over the world to attend conferences on women's issues. Given all these privileges, it is perhaps not surprising that they are so reluctant to give up their positions and return to anonymity. The leaders and members of these women's organizations remain predominantly middle- and upper-class, leaning towards a close collaboration with the government. This is perhaps most noticeable with the ICS and the WCSS. The former was founded by the wife of the Prime Minister, and the latter shifted from a voluntary association to a semi-governmental organization.

On the other hand, there has been a noticeable change in the activities (see Table 2, p. 112) of the women's groups: they have become more oriented towards educating women and providing services, rather than acting as pressure groups to bring about changes in women's status. They offer classes in Asian and Western cuisine, dressmaking, embroidery, foreign languages and Islamic studies. They also organize leisure activities and provide charity for the poor of Africa and Kuwait. These kinds of activities are 'important symbolic statements about class',[34] in the sense that they are expressions of class culture. To learn to speak French and English and to cook Western dishes, or to provide charity, forms part of a class repertoire, with its own particular practices and lifestyle.[35]

These activities are also highly political, in the sense that they act as mechanisms for the defence and reproduction of class relations. Many studies of women's groups have shown that these types of activities serve class interests more than they serve women.[36] Indeed, doing charity work or running cookery classes can do little to improve the situation of women; but, as many researchers have pointed out, philanthropy is part of a process through which the upper classes reproduce themselves. It keeps the lower classes under control and helps to maintain the *status quo*. Furthermore, to teach women how to speak French, how to bake a cake or how to sew serves only to reinforce their traditional roles rather than challenging the gender relations which form the basis of kinship relations.

Table 1. Example of a Worship Chart

Name . . . .

		Dawn		Morning duties		*Nawafil*	Work					Duties	Evening duties		Notes
Date	Day	Time	Duration	*Istighfar*	Quran		Office work	Islamic studies	*Figh*	*Hadith*	Housework	Islamic studies	*Istighfar*	Quran	

Nawafil Additional prayers. *Istighfar* Seeking God's forgiveness. *Figh* Islamic jurisprudence. *Hadith* Sayings of the Prophet Muhammad.

Table 2. Primary Activities of Contemporary Women's Societies

	Women's Cultural and Social Society	*Girls Club*	*Islamic Care Society*	*Bayader al-Salam*
Total membership (1990)	92	1,467	93	200
Activities	Cookery classes Adult literacy classes Care of cancer patients Funding orphanages Distribution of *zakat* Tea parties Lectures	English classes French classes Sporting activities Lectures	Quranic reading classes Dressmaking Embroidery Cookery classes Visiting orphanage Lectures	Religious seminars Distribution of *zakat* Lectures

5
The Politics of Contemporary Women's Organizations

The previous chapter has shown that, contrary to common belief, the women's societies in Kuwait are more than just a public place where women can get together to gossip and kill time. They are much more complex organizations located at the nexus of kinship structures, the class system, and other political forces present in the wider society.

This chapter examines the way in which the role of women in society has been defined and the kind of expectations, beliefs and norms that the women's organizations seek to generate and promote. In Kuwait, the women's organizations enjoy great authority over their members and strongly influence the way women's place is defined in society. This is because they are legally recognized as the only legitimate forum for women to engage in public activity and to express themselves; it is also because they hold legitimate means of communication which give them the authority to speak publicly to women and to influence their lives.

Therefore, to examine the way women's issues are conceptualized is to draw attention to the politics of women's organizations. Two main questions arise. First, are women's organizations serving the interests of women? Second, to what extent do the value systems that they generate differ from that of the contemporary Islamic movement? The ideology of the Islamic movement will be taken as the frame of reference within which to assess the position of women's organizations, because the Islamic movement has positioned itself against the feminist movement and has generated a new definition of womanhood which has become fairly widespread.

This chapter is divided into three sections. The first section examines the Islamic revival movement and its conception of women and the way in which Kuwaiti women have responded. The second section focuses on how the women's organizations have defined the role of women in society and compares it to that of the Islamic revival movement. The third section looks at the relationship between the state and the women's organizations, examining the major issues which dominated the public debate in the 1980s.

The Islamic Revival in Kuwait and the Women's Issue

Until the mid-1970s the Islamic revival in Kuwait, a predominantly Sunni country, was confined to a small group of men. Concerned about the decline in religious values, they advocated a return to an Islamic order. The founder of the Salafiya movement, Abdul Rahman Abdul-Khaleq, had a small number of male followers who gathered to listen to his sermons at the mosque where he worked as a *mullah* (preacher). The Ikhwan, who represent the Muslim Brotherhood movement, had attracted a larger number of people, but were then virtually overpowered by the nationalist groups. In 1980 the Islamic revival movement began to grow and to win the support of both men and women. For the first time, Kuwaiti women were to be recruited as *da'iyas*.

The male revivalists mainly aimed to restore a moral order, that is, to fight alcohol, drug abuse and *zina*. They pressed the government to ban nightclubs and to impose stricter segregation between the sexes in public places. The issue of the woman's role in society had received far more attention than any other issue. Never before, in such a short span of time, had so many books on 'women's duties in Islam' been published.[1] It was as if the Muslim revivalists wanted to wipe out, refute and delegitimize a century of nationalist writings on women's rights.

It was women, rather than thc government, who were the primary target of the Muslim revivalist movement. As Mernissi says, the entire foundation of Arab society was shaken by the very fact that 'Arab women had dared to speak out, to have an opinion of their own, to analyse and interpret events and to make certain demands'.[2] Indeed, for the first time in history, Arab women emerged as an autonomous group, capable of making claims on men and of acting independently from them. It is the way women fought for their rights that provoked real panic among men.

In his book *al-Da'wa al-Islamiya fi al-Kuwayt* (Islamic Preaching in Kuwait), al-Hassawi, a Muslim revivalist, acknowledged the fact that the early women's movement in Kuwait both angered and frightened men, and that it was for this reason that men welcomed and even encouraged the revival of Islamic beliefs and norms:

> From the very beginning, the women's movement in Kuwait took a radical stand. Some women dared to burn their *abbaya* in the schools. Then the call to lift the veil began to spread. Later, the leaders began to increase their attacks on Islamic precepts, calling on women to free themselves from all bonds. . . .Many of the conservative men stood with astonishment and dismay like a baffled person who is unable to move. They thought this was a sweeping movement that no one perhaps could stop; so they remained silent, albeit disapprovingly. No sooner had the Islamic movement emerged than the *hijab* began to spread. . . . The false propaganda which tried to show Islam as being an oppressive religion collapsed, and the lies of the leaders of the women's liberation movement were disclosed. . . . No one any longer listens to what they say.[3]

To undermine the women's rights movement, it was important for the male revivalists to portray it as false and un-Islamic. Anything that attacks or contradicts Islam is the ultimate expression of *kufur* (religious infidelity), which must immediately be denounced and stopped. For this reason, they went so far as to claim that the women's emancipation movement was part of an imperialist plot aiming to weaken and destroy the Islamic faith. As al-Hassawi argued:

> The campaign for the liberation of women led by some Kuwaiti women who have studied abroad is an extension of the movement for the liberation of women championed by Qasim Amin. It is a false campaign seeking to free women from safe and lawful bonds, and to draw them into public life under the pretext of not paralysing half of the community and of bringing women out of their imprisonment. Yet its true aim is to allow men to take pleasure at their sight in public gatherings, discos and public places as they have stripped themselves of their chaste clothes. Originally, this campaign was a masonic movement led by the Jews to destroy non-Jewish communities in order to rule the world.[4]

The subordination of women to men and to the family structure constitutes the essence of the Islamic community, and it is believed to be vital to its unity and survival.

Women's quest for autonomy also met strong criticism from Abdullah al-Nafissi, a former professor at Kuwait University and an active supporter of

Jam'iyat al-Islah (the Muslim Brotherhood organization). In a lecture delivered to a female audience on 27 March 1984, al-Nafissi argued that the women's movement in Kuwait was wrong to isolate itself from men and to 'put women against men':

> Leaders of the Arab women's movement have committed numerous errors. The most common has been to address the women's problem in terms of 'men against women'. . . . The emphasis should be placed upon the co-operation between men and women, and not on rivalry, competition and hatred [of men]. After all, we are pious people; we do not accept the separation of religion from the affairs of the state.[5]

Al-Nafissi also criticized Arab feminists for putting too much emphasis on female education. He argued that illiterate women play a more positive role in society than educated women. This is because education in the Arab world, which is based on Western models, has made Arab women 'selfish and individualistic—like Westerners—seeking their own personal happiness and not striving to serve society and solve its developmental problems such as the awakening of women'.[6] By 'awakening', al-Nafissi meant the development of an Islamic consciousness.

For the Muslim revivalists, as we have already seen, the imitation of the West is *kufur.* This is because the West is the 'enemy of Islam' and, with its values of sexual liberty, individualism and female autonomy, seeks to corrupt and destroy the Muslim community. Quoting Seyyed Qutb in his book entitled *al-Mar'a fi al-Islam* (Women in Islam), Sheikh Ahmad al-Qatan, one of the most popular *imams* in Kuwait, wrote:

> [Islam] aims to create a pure society where desires are not stirred up every second. . . . The betrayed gaze, the erotic move, the display of charm, the naked body: all those lead to nothing more than the arousal of bestial desires, to the release of the reins of nerves and will, to chaos that cannot be confined.[7]

For social chaos to be controlled, al-Qatan holds, women need to conceal their femininity and to avoid mixing with men. Drawing upon Quranic verses, male revivalists argued that Islam asked women to be modest and not to display their charms. Everything in a woman, it is said, is *aura* (sexual): her voice, her walk, her arms, all the parts of her body, except her hands and face, excite men and arouse desire.

The view of women as sexually dangerous draws on a long tradition of men's fear of women's sexuality, a tradition which is particularly strong in the Arab Muslim world. According to Mernissi, Muslim society rests on the firm belief that woman is *fitna*, 'the epitome of the uncontrollable, a living representative of the dangers of sexuality and its rampant disruptive potential'.[8]

To support the Islamic view of women as sexually dangerous and destructively charming, some male revivalists have gone so far as to falsify history. For example, al-Qatan argues that 'the fall of Greek civilization was caused by women's dazzling display of charms, their associations with men and their excessive *tabaruj* [adornment] and promiscuity'.[9]

Muslim revivalists have made *zayy al-Islami* (Islamic dress) the symbol of the Islamic movement, arguing that while it hides femininity it bestows upon women a sense of dignity and respect. Islamic dress consists of a *hijab* (scarf to cover the head and neck) and a loose dress to hide the shape of the body. Some religious scholars recommend wearing an additional cloak to wrap the body so that the head and shoulders are well concealed.

But if co-operation between men and women is considered essential, sexual equality is a different matter. Revivalists reject the notion of equality between the sexes. They claim that men and women have been created biologically different in order to fulfil different roles in society, and that God has given men alone the responsibility for providing for the family. They place their arguments on the following Quranic verse:

> Men are the protectors and maintainers of women, because God has given the one more [strength] than the other, and because they support them from their means. Therefore righteous women are devoutly obedient, and guard in [their husband's] absence what God would have them guard.[10]

The primary role of women is to be mothers: it is for this role that they have been created and why they have been given a more gentle, affectionate nature than men. In the words of al-Qatan:

> They [religious scholars] consider women, by virtue of their physical constitution, as naturally disposed to bear the role for which they have been created: that is, the role of motherhood, of bearing and rearing children. This role gives women a more emotional nature. In addition, a woman is faced with a menstruation cycle which occurs every month and all year round and which weakens her, reduces her ability to make up her mind, to express her opinions and to defend herself. For this reason, the Shari'a has built upon the natural differences between men and women, and differentiated between the sexes in many laws. It made men the protectors of women and gave men alone the right to divorce. Women

> are forbidden to travel without a *muharam* [male relative] or a husband or a trustworthy group even if it is for the *hajj*. It gave women the duty to care for children and ordered men to attend the congregational Friday prayers and to participate in *jihad* [holy war].[11]

Hence the differences between the sexes—differences which, it is claimed, are biologically rooted—are both natural and sacred since they reflect God's will. Women were created constitutionally different from men. Women menstruate and bear children, while men do not. Consequently, the family is the natural domain of women in which they are maintained and cared for by their husbands.

Male revivalists claim that Islam gives men absolute authority over women. Women are advised not to contradict, defy or rebel against men. This claim is often justified by the Quranic verse:

> As to those women on whose part ye fear disloyalty and ill-conduct, adominish them [first], [next] refuse to share their beds, [and last] beat them [lightly]; but if they return to obedience seek not against them means [of annoyance].[12]

For women to work in the wage sector is considered 'unnatural', unnecessary and disruptive. The revivalists have repeatedly argued that it is because women have neglected their natural role to compete with men in the wage sector that there has been an increase in delinquency, divorce and *zina*. A woman's place is in the home, looking after her family. Women are advised to give priority to their domestic duties. Nothing is believed to be more 'honourable', 'respectable' and 'noble' than a woman's role as mother and housewife. This role must not be neglected, even to pursue a career.

The revivalists are, however, not totally opposed to a woman working outside the home. What they advocate is the confinement of women to traditional jobs in sex-segregated institutions where competition with men is avoided. As Sheikh Muhammad Iman bin Ali al-Jami explains:

> We do not say—as many believe—that women should not leave the home to work. On the contrary, it is possible for a Muslim woman to work and she has ample opportunities to do so. . . . The Muslim woman can pursue her work but without competing, mingling or being in *khelwa* [alone in a separate room] with men. She can be employed as a teacher, a director or a secretary in a girl's school; or as a doctor, a nurse or a clerk in a women's hospital, or in other jobs which are most suited to her nature.[13]

It appears that what the revivalists want is to suppress and reduce the effect of female competition in the labour force and to ensure that male authority and privilege are maintained. Because they see women as competitors, the revivalists are trying to draw them into sex-segregated areas where they will serve women and compete against other women in less rewarding and primarily service-type jobs.

The claim that sexual inequalities are rooted in biological differences created by God provides irrefutable justification for relegating women to the domestic sphere and excluding them from the competitive world of the labour market. Whenever men have needed to control women and exclude them from the sphere of knowledge and organized labour, they have stubbornly put forward the ideology of biological differences. In nineteenth-century England, for example, when women began to pose a threat to male privilege in the public sector, the male reaction was similar to that of the contemporary Muslim revivalists. Western men generated a whole body of discourse to justify women's inability to compete in their male rational world. It was claimed, for example, that women lack the scientific skills required to become doctors.[14] What the Muslim revivalists wanted, however, was not simply to exclude women from the world of politics and organized labour. They also wanted to restore the absolute authority of men which the women's movement had threatened to disrupt.

The Islamic movement generated massive support from the very women who were, paradoxically, its primary target. In Kuwait, women joined the Islamic movement in their thousands. They discarded their Western clothes, wore the *hijab* and became the most loyal supporters of the Ikhwan and Salafi groups. Why were women so eager to join a movement which offers them nothing more than a subordinate and limited role confined to housekeeping and being of service to the female community? A complete answer to this question would fill another book, but I offer one suggestion. As will be explained in more detail below, the ideology of the Islamic movement (or, more precisely, the way the movement has presented itself to women), combined with the new avenues it opened up to women (i.e. a spiritual quest and/or militancy), offered new solutions to women who faced personal and cultural crises.

The feminist writer Maria-Antonietta Macciochi has explained fascism's appeal to women in Italy. Her argument is that 'fascism enlists the support of women by addressing them in an ideological–sexual language with which they are already familiar through the discourses of bourgeois Christian ideology'.[15] In a parallel way, Muslim revivalists have addressed themselves to women in 'an ideological–sexual language', using pre-existing religious and social ideology.

Both movements have used traditional religious sanctions to sanctify and glorify the family and the role of women within it. The family is placed at the centre of society, and women are held to be its moral guardians and protectors. Not only the family but the entire society is held to be dependent upon women's conduct. Women are the mothers and educators of the future generation. While motherhood is valued, femininity is devalued. In this remarkable symbolic combination, in which women are simultaneously *aura* and the guardians of morality, male revivalists define women as both sexual and moral beings and confer upon them a superior moral status. The effect of this artificial superiority is further reinforced through the constant use of concepts such as dignity, respect, honour and nobility to define women's position in Islam. Furthermore, Islam is represented as the 'authentic' way of life for all Muslims, men and women alike. The Islamic movement proposed a return to 'cultural authenticity', offering a more clearly defined identity to women torn by the issue of cultural betrayal.

Caught between two cultures, Western and Arab-Islamic, many merchant-class women were struggling to find a new meaning in their lives. The remark made by a Bayader member ('I felt lost; every day I did the same thing. I just put on different clothes; it was meaningless') was characteristic of the experiences of these women. Their Western education contradicted the expectations and values of their own society. In its spiritual dimension, Islam gave new meaning to their lives, without conflicting with their class interests.

Among the middle stratum, many women were growing resentful of the privileges and affluence of the upper classes. Kinship barriers prevented middle-class women from gaining access to privileged positions. Upper-class women controlled the women's organizations, had access to the most prestigious jobs, wore the most fashionable clothes and drove the most expensive cars. The degree of affluence marked the boundaries between social classes and reinforced class differences. In this context, Islamic dress was seen as a negation of class differences, and thus provided immediate relief from the distress these distinctions caused.

The Islamic groups also gave women new political aspirations. Women took an active part in the *da'wa* (preaching), lobbying, leafleting and organizing for the Islamic cause. They felt they were involved in making history, not their own, but that of the Islamic *umma* (community). This feeling of being part of history, rather than the marginal, inactive outsiders they had previously been, gave middle-class women a sense of worth and a new sense of 'being'.

The women who joined the Salafi and Ikhwan groups spoke the same language as men and believed in a similar interpretation of the Quran:

> We believe that women are the principal cause of that state [the disintegration of the Muslim community]. The moment that women departed from their childcare duties, dropped the Quran and became preoccupied with futile social activities, the *umma* began to weaken. . . Women are indeed placed in a very dangerous position. If they are corrupted the entire society becomes corrupted; and if they are righteous the society will stand upright and prosper.[16]

Female revivalists, however, went much further than men. They saw their roles as giving advice and converting women to Islam, and making them good Muslims. They wrote extensively, holding religious discussions and organizing many conferences on the issue of women and Islam. Their writings dealt with three main issues: the role and duties of Muslim women; *sifat al-mar'a* (female qualities); and *adab al-mar'a* (women's good manners). The aim was to teach women about their role and duties and to bring about a 'new Muslim woman'. Women were told that their primary responsibility was to be mothers and housewives, that they were indispensable to the family and that neither their maids nor their husbands could ever replace them.[17]

Women were also advised to obey their husbands. An influential woman called Teiba al-Yahia wrote, 'The husband is a generous prince . . . a good guardian. By law, the prince has to be obeyed within the limits of God's obedience.'[18] This statement appeared in a tract entitled *Wajibat al-Mar'a al-Muslima* (The Duties of the Muslim Woman), issued by the female students of the University of Kuwait, which aimed to help women understand their Islamic duties better. In discussing the relationship of wives to husbands, al-Yahia gave the following advice to married women on 'how to get closer to your husband's heart':

> 1. *A refuge*. God has described the wife as a refuge. . . . Hence, the refuge must be calm, pleasant to one's eyes, restful for the self [*nafs*]. . . . For this reason, the wife carries enormous responsibilities; that is, she has to make of herself a refuge in which her husband can rest. . . . Tired as he is, she should only receive him with a smile, greetings and joy. She should bless him and wish him good health. Such a warm reception will ease his hardship.
> 2. *Devotion*. For love to grow, a wife has to devote herself to her husband . . . to love him . . . *to put his interests ahead of hers* . . . to give his comfort priority over hers . . . to be calm and cheerful . . . and never to fail to make every effort to serve him.
> 3. *Devotion to his family and relatives*. To love your husband means also

> to love his family, his brothers and sisters . . . to be good to them . . . to be their companion . . . to be kind to them. . . . A husband may neglect, or simply forget about, his family duties; . . . the wife should be like a clock, always ready to remind him of his duties towards his family.
> 4. *Altruism.* A wife ought to overcome her selfishness . . . to control her feelings . . . to seek her husband's consent . . . *to give up some of her comfort and rights* for his sake . . . with pleasure, satisfaction and affection . . . without making him feel obligated.
> 5. *Giving gifts.* Giving gifts is also part of loving. A wife has to accept her husband's present with open arms . . . joy and jubilation . . . no matter how cheap or of poor quality the gift is. To receive a gift should be enough to bring jubilation and joy . . . He might have wished to give it to her because of a special occasion, or for other reasons, or he just wanted to give it to her because perhaps he thought the gift would be suitable.[19] [Emphasis added]

Hence women are asked to put the interests of their husbands above their own interests. Sacrifice, obedience, patience and complacency are considered the *sifat* (qualities) of the good Muslim woman. Meanwhile, women's *adab* (good manners) means modesty, chastity, wearing the *hijab*, and avoiding being in *khelwa* (alone with men) and committing *zina.*

The rights of women do not occupy a central place in these writings. When the issue is raised, it is often discussed in relation to what Islam has defined as women's rights and not in relation to women's actual needs. Female revivalists argue that Islam has given women the right to education, the right to be supported financially and the right to enter into business transactions, and that Muslim women should not attempt to claim more rights than those they have already received from Islam. The belief in biological differences makes the notion of equal rights meaningless.

Unlike men, female revivalists do not regard men as superior to women. Men and women are considered to be equal but different: equal because they have similar obligations towards God and different because they were created to fulfil different roles. As the president of the women's committee of the Kuwait National Union of Students (KNUS) expressed it:

> It is like night and day. Night does not precede day nor does day precede night; hence women are not superior to men, nor are men superior to women. Each sex has its own roles and responsibilities in this world and any interchange of roles will upset the order of life.[20]

The Women's Organizations and the Role of Women

The changes in the activities of the women's organizations were followed by the development of a new set of values which were very similar to those propagated by the Muslim revivalists. These values rested upon sexual morality and the complementarity of gender roles. In this way of thinking, the relationship between the sexes is based upon irreconcilable differences which are fundamental to a social and moral order, and women are responsible for maintaining this order. Bayader called on women to seek a spiritual life and to be chaste. The ICS defended women's domestic role and advised women to return to their homes. The WCSS and the Girls Club pleaded for a much wider range of female involvement in the labour force and, at the same time, placed a high value on sexual differences, family relations and moral conduct.

Bayader: a Community of Women and of Spiritual Realization

The essential difference between Islam as a religion and Islamic spirituality (*tasawwuf*) lies, as Seyyed Hussein Nasr puts it, 'in the dimension of depth or inwardness'.[21] Islamic spirituality deals with the esoteric (*batin*) dimension of Islam; it is connected with the world of the spirit (*ruh*). It should not, however, be confused with spiritualism *(zar)* or other experiences of spiritual possession. In Islam, human nature is considered to consist of *ruh* (spirit), *nafs* (soul) and *jism* (body). According to the Quran, God has 'breathed into man his own spirit'.[22] On the basis of this divine revelation, Sufis seek to get to the knowledge (*ma'rifa*) of God, and to realize *tawhid* (union with God). The achieving of *tawhid* is the essence of Sufism.

In order to reach unity with God, the Sufis have developed a spiritual discipline known as the *tariqa* (mystical path). As noted earlier, the *tariqa* may differ from one Sufi order to another, but the principle remains the same. The *tariqa* is a process of *tazkiyat al-nafs* (self-purification) and of acquiring divine virtues: patience, repentance, humility, charity, chastity, truthfulness, piety and *tawakkul* (absolute dependence on God). For this reason, as Saadia Khawar Khan Chishti, a well-known Pakistani scholar and follower of mysticism, has pointed out, '*tasawwuf* [Islamic mysticism] is appropriately called the science of purity of the human soul, and those who adhere to it live a purely virtuous life based on the Shari'a'.[23]

Perhaps the most important aspect of Sufism is the recognition of equality between men and women in their spiritual quest.

According to Chishti:

> As human souls, both the male and the female are absolutely equal in their relationship with the Creator; and as Muslims, both the male and the female need to cultivate the same virtues and perform the same Islamic rites, and before God they bear the same accountability for their actions.[24]

The Sufis accept the idea that men and women are created biologically different in order to undertake specific duties and responsibilities in their earthly life. However, unlike orthodox Islamic groups such as the Salafi and the Ikhwan, Sufis do not focus on sexual differences, nor does Bayader al-Salam. The difference between the women of Bayader and the members of the Salafiya and Ikhwan groups can best be understood in terms of the 'merger self' and the 'seeker self'. The 'seeker self' is involved in the process of inward self-transformation, whereas the 'merger self' is involved in serving others. Ursula King, an authority on religion, explains the difference:

> Women are so accustomed to living for others, whether partners, husbands, children or aging relatives, that they frequently subordinate their own identity and self to the needs and interests of other people. Their service to others, to their loved ones, which is so much needed for the maintenance of community, has in practice often developed into a caricature of true service by becoming excessive female subservience with the result of women's own spiritual deprivation. Such female subservience has often been encouraged by religious and spiritual authorities who have helped to condition women into what has been called a 'merger self' rather than to foster and nourish a 'seeker self'. But in order to grow to maturity women have to make their own journey along the spiritual path and undertake their own vision quest to answer the call of spirit.[25]

As practised in Kuwait, and perhaps in other parts of the Muslim world, mysticism can be seen as a new form of protest against patriarchy. The women of Bayader, for example, while remaining devout Muslims, were able to form a female community and escape from male control. The concept of *jama'a* (companionship), which is central to all Sufi orders, gave a new meaning to these women's relationships with each other. It helped to reinforce the exclusive character of female friendship and created stronger ties between women. It also helped the expression of emotions between them. But it is important to stress here that the concept of *jama'a* should not be confused with that of sisterhood in the feminist sense, because *jama'a* does not imply the love of all women but rather the love of some women. That is, *jama'a* is the love of Muslim women and of those with whom one has established a spiritual commitment.

It could be argued that Kuwaiti women have, in the past, lived separately from men, shared each others' difficulties and joys, created a community of their own, and used the *zar* and other methods of spiritual possession to find new power within themselves. Given this background, what makes Bayader so different? First, the physical separation from men at Bayader is a voluntary choice rather than one forced upon them by men. Second, kinship ties do not form the main basis of solidarity between these women. But perhaps more important, the difference can be seen in the way the women of Bayader have interpreted the woman's role in Islam and the way they have chosen to lead their lives, which represents an interesting new Islamic challenge to patriarchy.

Bayader contests the idea that the place of Muslim women is in the home, serving their husbands, doing the housework and bringing up the children. For them, motherhood is a natural female responsibility; but to confine women solely to the task of mothering, on the pretext of it being a natural role, and to define women's duties in relation to their husbands' needs alone is a 'distortion' of Islam. The leader of Bayader stated:

> The internal conflict and limitations which face Muslim women derive from the distorted Islamic image of woman's role. Women are conceived of as nothing more than a mere unfortunate instrument destined to rear children and to simply serve the men. This is a distorted Islamic view of women. Islam has honoured women and given them very high positions. Take Khadija, for example—she was the first to embrace Islam; or Umm Aymen, Aisha, and many other early Muslim women.[26]

What all these early Muslim women have in commmon is that they led a spiritual life devoted to God and Islam.

In seeking to lead their lives like the early Muslim women and the female saints who have played an important role in Islamic history, the women of Bayader shifted their object of devotion. They substituted the love of God for the love of men. Worshipping God and preaching Islam became the most important aspects of their lives. One of the married leaders said that she was happy now that she no longer had to cook for her husband and had left the task entirely to the cook. Another expressed her relief when her husband agreed to leave the shopping to the maid. She explained that when her husband first learned that she had sent her maid to the supermarket, he became very upset; she then told him that if she were to go instead she would end up buying more than they needed and this is *haram* (forbidden) in Islam. Then he was convinced. What is interesting about these two examples is that, in both cases, the reinterpretation of Islam has enabled married women to find legitimate ways of defying patriarchal authority and its conception of their domestic role. In this sense, the way the women of Bayader have chosen to lead their lives can be seen as a new form of challenge to patriarchy and to the male conception of woman's role in Islam.

It is Sufism, more than orthodox Islam, which gives women the legitimate means to reinterpret their roles. Mysticism gives them new power but, as King puts it, 'not power *over* but power *for*, enabling power, to seek spiritual, personal and social freedom which entail[s] further power for advising, teaching, writing, counselling, and helping others as well as power for building and transforming communities'.[27] In other words, they have found the power to change their lives.

Although this may make Bayader sound like a newly found heaven for women, one should be careful not to romanticize or misrepresent the impact of Sufism on women's lives. At Bayader, the upward displacement of the object of desire (i.e. from men to God) has led to a sublimation of sexuality. Sexual activities, from masturbation to penetration, are viewed as 'bestial' acts. Bayader holds that sexuality should be directed towards the only function for which it has been created: reproduction. The condemnation of sexual pleasure as a worldly concern can take repressive forms. For instance, a member who confessed to her *murshida* that she had masturbated was severely reprimanded and was asked to leave the group and not to return to Bayader until she had stopped her 'filthy' habits.

Many of Bayader's leaders have chosen to lead a celibate life in order not to be distracted from their devotion to God by worldly desires. Asceticism is not encouraged in Islam, but for many female mystics, 'the adoption of a celibate life gave them an independence and freedom in the exercise of religious life'.[28] What does this imply for those of Bayader's leaders who are married? I have often heard them speaking of sexuality in terms of 'duty' rather than personal plcasure. They have sexual intercourse with their husbands not because of any inner desire, but out of fear of being disobedient to God: Islam orders women to obey their husbands. A woman's refusal to satisfy her husband's sexual needs is in itself an act of disobedience which Muhammad has decreed should be severely punished. The Prophet is reported to have said, 'When a husband calls his wife to his bed and she refuses to come, the angels curse her until morning,' and 'Every wife who spends the night at the side of her satisfied husband is sure to go to paradise.'[29]

The whole Bayader system is based upon sexual morality, and the affirmation and imposition of Islamic *adab* which takes the form of rigid puritanism. It is considered *haram* (unlawful) for a woman to swim in a bathing costume, to be involved in any sporting activities, to dress provocatively or to go to the cinema. The ideal woman is the one who fears and loves God and who always does *al-amal al-salih* (virtuous deeds).

The Islamic Care Society and the Ideal Woman

When the ICS came into existence, it was to establish some order within a public sphere torn between the passive retreat into Sufism and the outward militancy of the Ikhwan and Salafiyin. Its aim was to promote a more moderate Islamic ideology. For this reason, the *hijab*, the symbol of the Islamic revivalist movement, was not encouraged by the ICS leaders. The image they wanted to disseminate was of the 'unveiled pious woman'. 'The ideal woman', explained an official, 'is one who works for the interests of society and the family, and seeks to do what benefits society; we need virtuous women and virtuous men who work loyally for their *watan.*' This statement is a neat summary of the ICS conception of the ideal role of women in society. Whereas the Islamic female revivalists want women to put men's interests before their own, the ICS leaders want women to sacrifice their interests for the sake of their *watan* and their family.

Like the Islamic revivalists, the ICS puts a strong emphasis on sexual differences. The idea that men and women are biologically different was particularly stressed in a report addressed to the government. 'God', according to the report, 'has created eternal biological differences between men and women, and the result of such differences is the unity represented by the family.'[30] On the basis of such assertions of biological differences, the ICS leaders tend to justify their demands for a sexual division of labour and for the restriction of women to traditional roles:

> We do want to encourage women to work and to take part in the labour force but provided only that such participation does not result in women's neglect of their families and of their childcare responsibilities, and provided also that they work in jobs which are most suited to their female nature. . . . We are against any kind of propaganda calling for the involvement of women in all kinds of jobs.[31]

The ICS leaders have been hostile to the WCSS in its call for the total integration of women in 'national development'. Domestic work, particularly the care of children, is considered to be a woman's primary responsibility. 'What is required', explained an official, 'is that women bring up good children who will not be a burden on the government; for this reason, it is better for women to stay at home and look after their children.'

The perception of women as 'naturally' fitted for domestic activities and not suited for men's jobs in the labour market is associated with the belief that gender inequality is not socially constructed but is rather a natural consequence of biological differences. Gender equality is therefore rejected under the claim that it is incompatible with the biological constitution of men and women. As an official put it:

> We do not believe in the equality between men and women because each sex has its own functions which are in harmony with its physical constitution; for instance, the profession of civil engineer is not suited for a woman because it requires that she go out in the field. We don't consider that there is any struggle between men and women; men are our husbands, fathers and brothers.

Of all the women's organizations, the ICS has shown the greatest concern for perpetuating women's traditional activities. The emphasis on sewing and embroidery is held to be part of an effort to 'revive women's heritage':

> Our main objective is to revive our heritage and to encourage it by all possible means. The most important of all are women's needlework activities which have existed in our beloved country, such as dressmaking and embroidery. That type of craft, which formed a major source of income for many families during the period of diving and trading, became a less desirable and less needed craft after the economic boom. The fact is that this is the most beautiful art; without it women's beauty will not be complete, and it is also the single most important way to add taste and elegance to the home and to a woman's personality.[32]

In the eyes of ICS members, dressmaking and embroidery are feminine activities which make women more attractive and enhance their femininity.

But is there not some other intent in this whole process of 'reviving tradition' to which women fall victim? Perhaps it is intended to give Kuwaiti society the sense of having a 'cultural identity', a kind of national 'heritage' which needs to be preserved. This process seemed particularly vital at a time when the Islamic revival movement was gaining strong popular support for its call for cultural authenticity.

The WCSS and the Girls Club: Who Needs a Women's Liberation Movement?
As described above, the Islamic revivalists aimed to refocus women's issues away from the conception of rights and towards that of duties; they also

wanted to prevent the development of a feminist consciousness. The leaders of the WCSS and the Girls Club, who witnessed the movement for equal rights for women, silently observed the development of an anti-feminist movement. They did little to oppose or even resist the Islamic movement. Their only protest was against the contemporary *hijab*: they argued that the Quran told Muslim women to be chaste and modest but did not order them to wear the *hijab*.

It is debatable whether the Quran imposed the veil on women in general, although it was imposed on the Prophet's wives. Muslim revivalists argue that since the veil was imposed on the Prophet's wives, the forebears of the Muslims, it goes without saying that all Muslim women should wear the veil. However, the Quran makes a clear distinction between the Prophet's wives and other devout women, and only in one *aya* (verse) does it mention the veil for ordinary women:

> Oh Prophet! Tell thy wives and daughters, and the believing women, that they should cast their outer garments over their persons [when abroad]: that is most convenient, that they should be known [as such] and not molested. And God is Oft-forgiving, Most Merciful.[33]

For many Muslims, this *aya* does not direct women to wear the veil. They argue that, during the time of the Prophet, women needed to veil when travelling in order to be recognized as members of the Muslim community and thus avoid being attacked.

What the WCSS and the Girls Club are opposed to is not the oppressive character of the practice of veiling, but the garment itself, that long, shapeless and unattractive cloak which reveals nothing more than perhaps a religious identity. In the early 1950s, when the young merchant-class women burnt their *abbayas*, it was to protest against their physical seclusion. Today the rejection of Islamic dress is linked to a desire to maintain their class identity, with all its signs of wealth and power. Thus, though they fiercely oppose the practice of veiling, they strongly support the Islamic *adab*, that is, female modesty, chastity and the avoidance of *zina*. Furthermore, they use their adherence to Islam to justify their attitude of complacency and resilience towards patriarchal society: 'We don't', explained a WCSS member, 'try to behave like Western feminists because for us religion and the state are not separate and if we try to change that, it is like being against God.'

By and large, they share the beliefs and ideas of the Islamic movement. They, too, support the idea that the sexual division of labour within the family is rooted in biological differences. A WCSS official was asked about the possibility of fathers staying at home to look after their children while their wives went out to work. Her reply was emphatic: 'No! Each sex has its role to play; you cannot shift responsibilities from one sex to the other.'[34] Such views are very common among members of the WCSS and the Girls Club. Women are held to be more emotional and patient than men, and 'because of their maternal instincts, are better suited to charity work'. The feminization of charity is, perhaps, the most significant impact that the WCSS has had on Kuwaiti women. More precisely, women have come to be seen as more skilful and better fitted than men for charity work and the general care of others. Charity work is construed as an extension of motherhood, that is, as a natural female activity that every Kuwaiti woman must aim to practise during her lifetime.

But, unlike the ICS and the Islamic groups, the WCSS and the Girls Club do not say that women should confine themselves to the responsibilities of childcare. Since the 1970s the WCSS has been campaigning for a much broader involvement of women in the labour market. The Regional Conferences on Women were designed to raise public awareness about the importance of women in the labour force and to press the Gulf governments to integrate women fully into national development. The 1981 and 1984 regional conferences focused specifically on women's role in development. WCSS leaders argued:

> Women's full participation in the development process is not a matter of superficially appearing to modernize the society, or a matter of imitating the advanced industrial societies; it is, rather, in its essence, a matter of civilized and sound development to liberate human beings—men and women—and to bring out their hidden abilities . . . and it [female participation] is not limited to women's civil and human rights; it implies women's obligations in fulfilling their duties.[35]

Women's work in the wage sector is held to be a 'national duty', with women urged to contribute to the full development of thcir country. 'It is of prime importance', argued the WCSS president, 'that greater attention be given to women's role in the family in terms of providing facilities and services in order to allow women to keep fulfilling their social responsibilities in the best possible manner.'

WCSS leaders want to ease government restrictions on the professional advancement of women. In 1980 the society addressed a petition to the Council of Ministers requesting that Kuwaiti women be appointed to senior government positions. Soon afterwards, educated women from well-established merchant families were appointed to posts such as assistant under-secretary and faculty dean. The fact that women were appointed to senior government posts was sufficient for the WCSS and the Girls Club to claim that Kuwaiti women had achieved all the civil rights guaranteed by the constitution and that there were no other rights worth fighting for, except perhaps the right to political participation. For example, members stated:

> Kuwaiti women have been given all their rights, and by comparison with women in other Gulf countries, Kuwaiti women are much better off. We have asserted ourselves. Thank God, we now have women in very important official positions. [Girls Club]

> There is nothing that a Kuwaiti woman feels that she is lacking or missing in her life. She has claimed all her rights, far more rights than American or European women. We took our rights because Islam has given us those rights. If we were to compare ourselves with Western women, thank God we could say that we have reached similar positions. What remains is to gain our political rights. [WCSS]

The women of the the WCSS go even further in refuting the idea that Kuwaiti women have ever been oppressed or subject to discriminatory practices. In a paper presented at the UN World Conference on Women in Nairobi in 1985, the WCSS president, Lulua al-Qitami, stated that 'women's role in the hard pre-oil era was a pioneering heroic one hardly witnessed in any other society'. She further argued that because their husbands were away so long on trading voyages, Kuwaiti women were in charge of everything: 'The woman was the minister of finance.' The WCSS president also claimed that the harsh and difficult circumstances:

> transformed the Kuwaiti woman into someone professionally capable of defying hardship, of creating and fostering family bonds and producing men capable of facing and enduring the hardships of life. . . . A historical background to the Kuwaiti woman's role in the family is necessary to understand her nature and her ability to endure, meet challenges and adhere to great aspirations.[36]

The Women's Organizations and the State

Throughout the 1980s the women's organizations established a strong and supportive relationship with the government, defending, promulgating and implementing its policies on the role of women in Kuwait. The government was anxious to bring women back to their traditional occupations, to divert their attention from feminist issues and to make them good and 'useful' citizens.

The government faced many new problems: a rising tide of Islamic revivalism, a weakening of family ties, increasing expenditure and general apathy towards their own country among Kuwaitis themselves. It turned to the women's organizations for assistance. The reason was simple: women are the main consumers of domestic goods, the sole providers of childcare and the mediators of kinship relations. In teaching women how to fulfil their family responsibilities for the benefit of society, the government hoped to solve some of its problems. Throughout the 1980s, therefore, the focus was on how to make women better mothers and more conscientious housewives. The WCSS and the Girls Club raised the issue of women's right to political participation but failed to have any impact on the prevailing male attitude towards women's role in the society.

The following section reviews the issue of women's suffrage and examines the response of the women's organizations to the government's call for women to return to their domestic duties.

The Demand for Political Participation

The issue of women's suffrage was raised in 1981, a year after the parliamentary system was restored. At that time, the government showed some interest in granting women the right to vote. In 1980, in a televised speech, Crown Prince and Prime Minister Sheikh Saad al-Abdullah Al Sabah stated, 'The time has come to take note of the position of the Kuwaiti woman and her effective role in society and put forward the matter of the vote for study and discussion.'[37] The matter was later raised by a parliamentary deputy, Ahmad al-Takheim, who presented a bill to the National Assembly requesting that articles 1 and 19 of the Electoral Law be amended so that women would be allowed to vote but not to hold office. The bill was discussed on 19 January 1982. The debate went smoothly and lasted only a few hours, but the bill was finally rejected 27:7 with 16 abstentions. Many deputies who had initially been in favour of giving women the right to vote preferred to abstain, fearing that to grant them such a right would tip the balance of power in favour of the Islamic groups.

The university experience had shown that it was the female students who gave the Ikhwan the power to control the KNUS—they had voted massively for the Ikhwan since 1978. It was also women who helped the Ikhwan control the Teachers Society and many other voluntary associations. It is not surprising that the Ikhwan, in contrast to the Salafiyin and the conservative *ulama*, were most in favour of giving women the right to vote. The Ikhwan claimed that Islam forbade women to govern or rule, but it did not exclude them from politics. It also claimed that in the past Muslim women had taken part in battle.

The influential role of women in the contemporary Islamic movement was acknowledged by an Islamic deputy who was arguing in the Assembly in favour of giving women the right to vote:

> The Islamic movement in this country will grow because all those who are calling for liberties and national issues are members of the Islamic trend. Therefore, if we allow women to participate in political decisions, this will mean the political growth of the Islamic movement.[38]

But the fear of such growth discouraged the government from further supporting women's suffrage; it preferred once again to remain neutral.

The rejection of the bill was met with a mixture of fury and joy. A group of women who were opposed to the bill gathered 1,000 signatures from women and sent the petition to the deputies with a letter of thanks. It read as follows:

> We, the undersigned, are pleased to raise our voice to you [Mr President] and to all those who have stood firmly against the bill, in support of its rejection. True believing Muslim women support the rejection [of the bill] and disapprove of any debauchery. We ask that the debate on this matter be closed for ever. We have great faith in our country and in our men. Under the present circumstances, to urge women [out of their homes] would give rise to many family problems, with consequences that cannot be praised. We all hope that our country will be secure and that women's rights will be maintained in accordance with our respected Shari'a.[39]

On the other hand, the Girls Club and the WCSS were furious at the rejection of the bill. The WCSS addressed a written complaint to the deputies.

Though the same bill could be raised only once during a session of the Assembly, the WCSS and the Girls Club were ready, the moment that the question of their political rights was raised, to fight back and gather more support for their cause. They organized public debates on the issue of women's political rights and wrote articles in the press, desperately seeking to win support from both men and women.

On 9 February 1982, when the chamber was scheduled to review the complaints, the WCSS president led a group of women to the Assembly.

They wanted to hear the deputies' comments and to demonstrate their anger. At the sight of these women, the deputies hurriedly filled the back seats, leaving the front seats empty. The complaints were briefly discussed. The deputies clearly wanted to avoid any kind of embarrassment or confrontation amongst themselves in front of so many women. Amused by the situation, one female activist wrote a newspaper article entitled, 'They Left their Seats and Fled'.[40]

As the 1985 elections drew closer, the Girls Club showed its support for the Tali'a group (Arab nationalists) and agreed to lobby for their candidates provided that, when elected, they would press for women's suffrage. The nationalists agreed. The Girls Club leaders formed the Organizing Committee for the Political Rights of Kuwaiti Women. The committee, which was composed of 12 active women, organized public debates, raised money for the Arab nationalists' campaign, contacted male students studying abroad and distributed pamphlets. The Arab nationalist candidates were invited to hold political debates at the club.

The WCSS leaders, on the other hand, did not strike a deal with the Arab nationalists. Instead, in February 1985, they went to the voter registration office to place their names on the electoral list, claiming that the denial of their voting rights was a violation of Kuwait's constitution. Officials at the registration office refused to accept their applications. Having been rejected, WCSS leaders tried to report the 'constitutional offences' to the police. Their grievances were again rejected.

Three of the Tali'a group and five other Arab nationalist candidates were elected, along with two Ikhwan candidates. But the bill to grant women the right to vote was not passed. It was blocked by the Assembly's Legal Affairs Committee whose members called on the Ministry of Awqaf and Islamic Affairs for a legal ruling.

On 24 July 1985 a *fatwa* (legal ruling) was issued declaring that, 'The nature of the electoral process befits men, who are endowed with ability and expertise; it is not permissible for women to recommend or nominate other women or men.'[41] The *fatwa* provoked an uproar. The Ikhwan protested. Their leader proclaimed, 'Islam says a woman should cover her hair and her arms, not her mind!'[42] A few months later, however, the National Assembly was suspended, mainly because the intense questioning of some cabinet members about financial issues led to the resignation of the Justice Minister.

From Political Rights to Motherhood: the Making of a Good Housewife

No sooner had the Assembly been dissolved than the women's organizations turned their attention to other issues. (The issue of women's suffrage in Kuwait has frequently been raised when the Assembly is in existence, but is then forgotten as soon as the Assembly is dissolved.) In the 1980s the main focus was on the questions of motherhood and family relations. There was a growing fear that traditional family ties were in danger of disintegration. The first to raise the alarm was the WCCS. As early as 1979 the society addressed a report to the Council of Ministers:

> The rapid economic changes have affected the stability of the family and its style of living. Kuwaiti women have entered the fields of knowledge, of work and of production. They have assumed, in joint collaboration with their men, responsibilities in modern urban institutions. Married women are no longer confined to the burden of the domestic sphere and to childcare, and their husbands are also extremely busy with the new economic enterprises. This has affected the competence of the family in childcare and reduced their engagement to it. To overcome this deficit, some families have resorted to foreign nannies. The latter come from various nationalities, speak different languages and hold beliefs and traditions very different from this society, posing a great danger to our Arabic-Islamic style of child-rearing and to the social *loyalty* of Kuwaiti children.[43] [Emphasis added]

In response to the perceived danger of foreign nannies, the WCSS proposed that the government should establish state-run nurseries with well-trained personnel. There, working mothers could keep their children away from the subversive influence of foreign maids and nannies. It was for this reason that the WCSS established a nursery as early as 1975 and hired qualified staff to provide good care for Kuwaiti children. The nursery was not meant to be a recreational place, where children under the age of 4 could develop their individuality and creativity. On the contrary, it aimed to make them obedient, family-oriented and loyal citizens. Children received an elementary religious education in which they were taught the importance of praying and fasting, and some basic Islamic *adab*, such as 'obedience, generosity, sincerity and hygiene'. Children also received a so-called 'social education' course which aimed to make them understand the meaning of kinship, neighbourhood, work and school.

The government acknowledged the danger of foreign nannies and was alarmed at the increasing number of non-Kuwaiti domestic workers: in 1981, it was estimated, each household in Kuwait had an average of two servants. The family has always been an important unit for the state. Article 9 of the constitution proclaims:

> The family is the cornerstone of society. It is founded on religion, morality and patriotism. The law shall preserve the integrity of the family, strengthen its ties and protect under its auspices motherhood and childhood.

In democratic societies run by an elected government, the relationship between family ties and patriotism is perhaps less marked. But in Kuwait, where political power is hereditary and in the hands of the Al Sabah family, the assimilation of the concept of family with that of *watan* is crucial to the perpetuation of the regime. This is why the government was always eager to promote the symbol of 'one family' (*al-usra al-wahida*) and to propose legislation to preserve family ties.

But a female workforce was important and necessary in a sex-segregated society, especially because of the Kuwaitization policy. Thus the government did not urge women to return home but instead supported the WCSS's idea of providing nursery facilities for working mothers. The issue of nurseries was included for the first time in the Five Year Plan for the period 1985/86–1989/90. It was stated as part of the human resources policy:

> To provide nursery facilities so that working mothers can reconcile the responsibilities of work and those of the family; and to encourage the private sector to build such facilities, following the example of the small number of model nurseries that the state is in charge of building.[44]

Nursery facilities were one possible solution to the problem. The government saw women in their role as mothers as an important vehicle for the transmission of social values. If children were to become loyal citizens, the mothers must be guided and taught about the society's values and needs. Recognition of the invaluable role of mothers in the transmission of values led the government to urge concerned state institutions and the women's societies to:

> take an interest in women's role as housewives, to enlighten women about society's problems and guide them, particularly, towards a sensible level of domestic consumption and the firm establishment of the society's values in childhood education.[45]

Bayader's leaders have long recognized the importance of the mother–child relationship and have placed a strong emphasis on educating children. The government appeal came as no surprise to them. Earlier, in 1984, they had held a public seminar on domestic consumption to teach housewives how to be more economical. Bayader also sought, in collaboration with other women's organizations, to reinforce the state belief that 'good women mean good nations', which became the most popular slogan of the 1980s in Kuwait.

The ICS held a series of seminars on family relations in Islam, and in December 1986 it organized a forum on mother–child relationships to which all its members were invited. The aim of the forum was to allow members to share their own childcare experiences and to help them develop better methods of controlling their children. The discussion centred round the following subjects: how to look after an infant; how to supervise your children's friends; how to follow up and supervise your children's studies; and finally, how to cultivate good habits in your children and train them to manage their daily activities.

It was the Girls Club that most helped to reinforce the ideology of maternal ignorance. In 1985 the organization began to question women's ability to fulfil their maternal role. As one officer argued:

> The only kind of training that women receive is job training. There is inadequate training for women in their roles as sisters, wives, mothers, and as active members of the society. We believe that even the delegation of childcare duties to servants is not due to affluence but to the *mother's ignorance* of the principles of childcare. This is an indication of 'social illiteracy'. Alphabetic literacy has not eradicated social illiteracy. Today, childcare requires a knowledge of the rules of hygiene, sterilization, and the mental and spiritual development of the child, etc. And all this is not so simple. [Emphasis added]

On 22 February 1987 the Girls Club launched its two-week intensive training course on motherhood and childcare. The course syllabus fell in line with the new trend of state policies designed to make women better mothers and more rational consumers. A total of 10 lectures dealt with the issues of childcare, foreign nannies, domestic consumption and family health. The importance of the mother–child relationship was repeatedly emphasized. Women were warned of the dangers of foreign nannies, advised to provide a balanced diet for their children to promote physical and mental growth, and constantly reminded of their primary reponsibilities in childcare.

Hence, once again, Kuwaiti women were to find themselves the subject of public debate. This time, it was their maternal role that was discussed, scrutinized and criticized. This role was claimed to be innate and natural on the one hand and, on the other, too much for a woman without proper training. This contradiction reflects the ideological basis of gender roles and the opposing but linked strategies of both the revivalists and the state. In order to ensure men's control over women, the revivalists needed to stress natural differences; meanwhile, for the state, motherhood is valuable for the role it plays in the transmission and reproduction of values. If mothers were to transmit the values of the society, they needed to be properly trained.

Caught between the state and the Muslim revivalists, women's societies defined their role in terms of educating, teaching and guiding women towards what they believed to be the 'right' path. Throughout the 1980s the societies constantly reminded women of their maternal role. Meanwhile, female revivalists campaigned intensively for prolonged maternity leave. Before its dissolution in 1986, the National Assembly agreed in principle to allow civil servants two years' maternity leave at half pay, in spite of the fact that such a move might prove extremely costly for the government.

Conclusion

In spite of their perceived political differences, Muslim revivalists and the contemporary women's organizations share a similar conception of femininity and masculinity. They claim that biological differences are the basis for the attribution and assignment of social roles. Because women bear children, they are unquestionably the providers of childcare. Men's main responsibility is to provide financial support for their wives and children.

In stressing social and biological differences, the women's organizations shifted from the issue of equal rights and perpetuated the belief that women are different from men, with their own specific needs and duties. Like the revivalists, they focused essentially on women's duties, defining areas of female responsibilities and urging women to be good housewives.

In promoting the idea that gender differences are the natural consequence of biological differences, rather than being socially constructed, the women's organizations have perpetuated the subordination of women to men. In other words, they have re-established the unequal system of gender relations and prevented women from seeing themselves other than in relation to men and to their family obligations. And it is precisely in dismissing the concept of women's autonomy and individuality that the women's organizations have contributed to the subordination of women, thus consolidating the patriarchal foundations of Kuwaiti society.

Conclusion

My primary aim in writing this book was to unravel some of the myths surrounding Arab women and highlight their ability to make decisions and to influence the course of action taken by male society. It is true that in almost every part of the Arab world, the situation of women appears almost immutable: early marriages, strict sexual norms, subordination to male authority and to the patriarchal family. Such rigidity in traditions and customs is by no means the result of Islam alone but rather a combination of political, economic and patriarchal forces—in other words, the politics of gender.

The Politics of Gender

My analysis of women's organizations in Kuwait reveals two important points. First, middle- and upper-class Kuwaiti women have no desire to change the traditional roles of women; on the contrary, they seek to maintain female dependence. Such complacency and acquiescence in gender attributes and roles contribute to the perpetuation of female subordination and the maintenance of the *status quo*. Second, gender politics are not only essential to class politics; they are also central to the mediation of political conflicts. This concluding chapter reviews these findings and asks whether there is any possibility for a female solidarity movement to emerge in Kuwait.

In Chapter 1, we saw that political power in Kuwait is shared by two groups: the ruling family and the closely related merchant class. For both groups, the tribal system of organization helped them to retain their economic and political power, and enabled them to evolve as a distinct group of *asil* (noble) origin. In spite of the changes in lifestyle that accompanied the discovery of oil, both groups maintained strong kinship networks. The importance of these kinship ties to political and economic organizations meant that any upset to the principle of family honour or to kinship loyalty might affect the stability of the ruling classes. It was for this reason that the merchant families, whose class power was made possible through the control of female sexuality, have clung so firmly to the concept of *sharaf* (honour).

The control of women's sexuality has been essential to the merchant class. It has served to maintain the purity of the lineage (i.e. the *asil* origin) and to preserve wealth and power within the family. During the pre-oil era, veiling and the strict seclusion of women, arranged marriages, and the principle of family honour which rested upon female chastity all operated as powerful mechanisms of social control. These kept women 'in their place' and ensured the reproduction of legitimate heirs. Though female seclusion and veiling were later lifted as part of the movement for *nahda* (awakening) and *taqaddum* (progress), women's sexuality continued to be firmly regulated through arranged marriages and the concept of family honour. Respectability became an important component of women's conduct. To be a respectable woman is to conduct oneself with modesty and virtue in relation to men. But despite a reinforcement of the value of respectability, the men of the merchant class were concerned that women might misuse their new alleged 'freedom'. The fear that their women might indulge in unlawful relationships with unrelated men weighed heavily on them. Thus they welcomed and even encouraged the establishment of women's societies, which would distract women and give them something useful to do.

Ironically, the women's organizations soon embroiled the ruling classes in a disturbing political conflict. In Chapter 3, we saw that the women's rights movement led by Nouria al-Sadani, which faced strong opposition from men, gave a great impetus to the Islamic revival in Kuwait. The movement to gain equal rights and to restrict polygamy was the first organized female challenge to men's power and privileges. It forced men to notice that women could act as an autonomous group and make claims on men by exercising political pressure. The support that the women's movement drew from the nationalist groups gave it considerable strength.

In its struggle to restore patriarchy, the Islamic revival set itself up as a political movement. It turned the Kuwaiti nationalists' ideology upside down. It spoke in terms of *asala* (authenticity) and *turath* (cultural heritage) rather than in terms of *nahda* and *taqaddum*. It also raised such controversial issues as national identity and the legitimacy of monarchist regimes in Muslim societies.

The government's response to the Islamic challenge was to adopt an Islamic stand and to present itself as even more Islamist than those who called themselves Muslim fundamentalists. Gender, which was at the centre of the political conflict, became an essential force for regulating that conflict. The government saw the women's organizations as a vital tool, not so much in perpetuating gender inequalities as in disseminating patriotic values and curbing the influence of fundamentalism. In the early 1980s the government closed the Arab Women's Development Society (AWDS) and licensed two Islamic women's organizations instead, thus marking the end of the women's rights movement. The ensuing shift, from demands for self-determination to those for female subjugation, clearly illustrates how issues of gender can be seized on and manipulated in the turmoil of political conflict.

Disunity and rivalry between the early women's organizations facilitated and even encouraged government intervention. The Kuwaiti Women's Union (KWU) failed when the Women's Cultural and Social Society (WCSS) and the AWDS fought with one another over its presidency. The Girls Club, which was established to give the AWDS more power within the KWU, actually deepened the rivalry between the women's societies and illustrated the inability of Kuwaiti women to unite in their struggle and agree on common aspirations.

The rivalry and mutual hostility between the early women's organizations reflect one of the many contradictions between gender and class. For the elite women, the protection of kinship interests and the maintenance of class power still override gender solidarity. The WCSS, which includes only the daughters of the most powerful merchant families, has shown very little concern with women's issues. In the 1970s, when Kuwaiti housewives who had been the victims of domestic male violence asked for help, they were turned down. The WCSS has been mainly concerned with 'the politics of status maintenance'.[1] The establishment of a nursery to teach children 'status-appropriate' language and behaviour in order to reinforce kinship loyalty, the provision of charity, and the arrangement of tea parties for the ambassadors' wives are all important activities of status maintenance.

What all the contemporary women's organizations have in common is the desire to maintain the *status quo*. In Chapter 5, we saw that throughout the 1980s the women's organizations supported the government and endorsed its views on women's issues. The majority of their leaders, who now belong to the merchant class and the ruling family, rejected what the AWDS had fought for, namely gender equality and women's autonomy. Though they continued to press for women's suffrage, there was an underlying consensus among these leaders that the asymmetrical relationship between men and women must be maintained—in other words, men rule and women obey. The primary duty of every woman was to be both a loyal citizen and a 'perfect' mother.

Even Bayader al-Salam, which presented an alternative form of protest against patriarchy, made no attempt to disrupt the existing power structure of the society. Bayader offered a kind of escapism from worldly concerns and substituted God for man, without attacking the roots of gender inequalities or even considering the uneven gender experiences rooted in daily practices. In ignoring the everyday reality of women's experiences, Bayader failed to deal adequately with gender issues or to confront patriarchy directly.

The political direction pursued by most of the contemporary women's organizations appeared to consist mainly of restoring patriarchy as a means of preserving the social order. Because a social change might threaten their privileges, it seemed vital for upper-class and elite women to bargain for gender inequality and female oppression in return for political stability. Kinship and class interests prevail over those of gender. The enthusiasm and dedication of the women's organizations to awakening patriotism echoed the government concept of *al-usra al-wahida* ('the one family'), which aimed to give a sense of cohesion and unity to a society torn by social and gender inequalities.

Perhaps the most important irony of the women's organizations in Kuwait is that the situation of women cannot be separated from the survival of the state. Gender and politics are so closely intertwined that to separate one from the other is to put the stability of the state at risk. The gender-based system of relationships supports a whole set of beliefs upon which the state is dependent. Kuwaiti women need to assume their traditional roles as mothers and housewives because the state needs motherhood. The more children Kuwaitis have, the more the indigenous population will increase and the less dependent the state will be on foreign workers. Hence the state offers financial incentives to encourage Kuwaitis to get married and have large families.

But women are not only important as mothers, that is, as producers of children and as transmitters of social values. They are also producers and mediators of kinship relations. The whole structure of the state is still based on kinship, along the lines of the tribal system of *ashira*. It is the centrality of kinship to the political organization which makes the situation of women in Kuwait, as perhaps in many Middle Eastern countries, appear to suffer from such a depressing state of inertia. More precisely, the position of women in their roles as mothers, wives and daughters cannot be altered significantly because any change in their traditional roles will threaten the existence of the state. In other words, any changes in gender relations or in women's status will inevitably require a reorganization of the political system, hence a dismantling of the kinship and patriarchal order. Neither the state nor the male community is willing to pay the costs of such a reorganization or even to begin searching for a compromise.

Whither Feminism in Kuwait?

The fundamental question that arises from this study is whether there is any possibility of a female solidarity movement emerging in Kuwait. As we have seen, both patriarchy and the social system, based as they are on unequal access to resources and privileges, contribute to setting women apart and obstructing the development of female solidarity. Furthermore, women are intimately related to the family and to kinship structures, not simply as wives, mothers and daughters but also as kin members; this situation constructs them 'ideologically, as having primary loyalties to these institutions'.[2] Kinship loyalty is particularly important for women of the elite classes: their class privileges will survive only as long as their kinship organization.

Such impediments to the development of a female solidarity movement have considerable implications for women in low-income groups. It is these women, perhaps more than any others, who suffer most from the discriminatory welfare policies of the state and from patriarchal structures, whether in the form of male violence or male religious discourse. Kuwaiti women from low-income families who violate the rules of sexual conduct are more likely to be arrested and imprisoned. Between 1986 and 1988, 42 women were arrested at the maternity hospital for giving birth to illegitimate children (abortion is illegal in Kuwait). Of these 42 women, 11 were jailed for more than 2 years, 17 were forced to marry their lovers, and 14 were put under the guardianship of male family members who pledged to the public prosecutor that such sexual misconduct among women in their families would not be repeated. During this 2-year period, there were at least 16 cases of rape, all of which were denied by the men allegedly involved. For men, the best way to avoid being found guilty is to deny knowing the women who stand accused of illicit sexual relations.

The issue of women's solidarity must be addressed if changes in the conditions of all Kuwaiti women are to occur. The women's organizations, which should have acted on behalf of all Kuwaiti women, have in fact spoken and acted on behalf of the elite. For a female solidarity movement to emerge will require the development of a gender-specific consciousness, that is, a 'women's consciousness'. This means an awareness of being a woman, sharing a common gender history with other women, and a willingness to raise gender issues and change the situation in favour of women. A gender-specific consciousness is not the same as a collective awareness of gender politics. For instance, as we have seen, the WCSS and the Girls Club were aware of the fact that Kuwaiti women were being discriminated against. Yet all they demanded was women's suffrage and professional advancement, issues that had no direct relevance to the everyday world of most Kuwaiti women. The emergence of a women's consciousness requires that women see themselves not as members of a class or as individuals, but as a 'collective social being'. If a female solidarity is to emerge in Kuwait, it is important that women begin to see themselves as a collectivity sharing a common fate and to raise a feminist consciousness based on their experiences as Arab and Muslim women.

Perhaps the basis for a female solidarity movement lies outside the formal women's organizations. In the seafaring Kuwaiti community, the informal ties among women helped them create ways of curbing men's power and of improving women's situation. They taught each other the Quran and engaged in *zar* ceremonies. In Africa and in many parts of Asia, women are organizing around a nucleus of informal associations which have proved to be highly effective in improving their situation and reinforcing gender solidarity.

Informal women's associations provide a means by which women can escape government control and raise gender issues. But in order to operate effectively, informal women's associations in Kuwait need to form a network, bringing together women from different strata in mutually supportive relationships. Communication links and solidarity between women across class lines are vital if they are to achieve desirable changes in their status. The basic similarities in their experiences as women can perhaps become a common ground from which women of the middle and lower strata can establish a dialogue. But first, Kuwaiti women need to give priority to women's interests and break away from their reliance on male discourse. As we have seen, many women of the middle stratum are caught up in the Islamic movement. It is only when they begin to question the male interpretation of Islam and to speak for themselves and about their shared experiences that it will perhaps be possible to expect the rise of a genuine female solidarity in Kuwait.

Postscript: the Situation of Women in Post-war Kuwait

On 2 August 1990 Iraqi troops invaded Kuwait. Thousands of Kuwaitis fled the country, the government went into exile and Kuwait was declared the 19th province of Iraq. For the next seven months, Kuwait was under the control of the Iraqi government. To liberate Kuwait, the UN Security Council ordered the use of force: war was declared on 17 January 1991. Iraqi troops fought back, setting the oilwells on fire. Kuwait was finally liberated on 26 February 1991.

In the aftermath of the Iraqi occupation, Kuwait began its long process of recovery amid political turmoil and a fragile economy. The occupation brought to the surface the dilemmas and problems that lay at the very heart of the political and social fabric of Kuwaiti society: the issues of democracy, the demographic imbalance between expatriates and the indigenous population, the gender gap and, finally, the *bedoun* (stateless citizens). The gap between expatriates and Kuwaitis was dealt with by introducing tougher immigration and employment measures. Work permits for thousands of expatriates were not renewed and very few were issued. As a result, for the first time in Kuwait's history the number of foreign workers, particularly those of Arab origin, employed in the private and government sectors dropped sharply. By 1993 the number of expatriate workers in Kuwait stood at 695,001 compared to 1,577,892 in 1990. The Kuwaiti population had risen from 578,454 in 1990 to 631,918 in 1993.[1]

Another pressing problem for the government was the restoration of the

National Assembly to appease the growing demand for political reform. Elections were held for the Assembly on 6 October 1992, with 278 candidates competing for 50 seats. Only Kuwaiti men over the age of 21 were allowed to vote. The opposition candidates, many of them tied to conservative Islamic groups, won 32 seats. The new parliament put high on its agenda three issues conceived as the most fundamental: the government's conduct leading up to the Iraqi invasion, Kuwait's foreign investments and the institution of the Shari'a as the sole source of legislation. Women's issues came very low on the agenda despite widespread recognition and praise for the role of women during the occupation.

Kuwaiti women responded with immense courage to the Iraqi occupation. On 6 August 1990 they marched into the streets of occupied Kuwait holding banners of protest against the invasion. The Iraqi soldiers fired at the demonstrators and two women were killed. This brutal incident did nothing to deter women from defying the Iraqi forces. Many women joined the resistance movement. They monitored roadblocks and passed information on troop movement and house searches. They edited underground newsletters and distributed food and money to neighbours and trapped foreigners. Some smuggled arms and fought with the resistance units. The Iraqis were aware of the women's sporadic activities, and consequently inflicted the same punishments on women as they did on Kuwaiti men. Hundreds of women were raped and tortured. Many others were killed or died as a result of torture or injury at the hands of the Iraqi soldiers.

Post-war Kuwait recognized women's patriotic stand but did nothing to improve their situation. In spite of many appeals from women themselves, the government remains reluctant to disturb the patriarchal order of Kuwaiti society. Women are to remain second-class citizens whose rights and obligations are circumscribed by their roles as mothers, wives and daughters. Women are first and foremost the moral guardians of the Kuwaiti family. Not only is it their duty to maintain family ties but also to spread the Islamic and social values of Kuwaiti society.

The ensuing recognition of Kuwaiti men as heads of families and as the sole breadwinners has left women, particularly those married to non-Kuwaitis, in a desperate condition. Of the 4,000 Kuwaiti women married to non-Kuwaitis who have submitted applications to obtain government housing since 1988, only a quarter have received their housing. Furthermore, the restrictions imposed on expatriates have deeply affected the lives of those Kuwaiti women married to non-Kuwaitis. Their foreign husbands are treated like any other expatriates: they have no legal rights in Kuwait and must leave the country if they cannot secure a residence permit. Residence is granted for a period of one year on condition of the approval of the Interior Minister, and is subject to renewal or termination. As to the children, they also have to apply for a residence permit in order to remain with their Kuwaiti mothers and are not entitled to the free medical care that other Kuwaitis enjoy.

After the war, the government made no attempt to provide jobs for the foreign husbands of Kuwaiti women. As a result, many were unable to secure work permits and were unemployed. Their wives went to work. Some took up jobs as *farrashas* (attendants) in girls' schools, others as primary school teachers receiving monthly salaries that were hardly sufficient to maintain the family. Such a situation angered these women. Why should the foreign wives of Kuwaiti men be entitled to enjoy all the rights and privileges of Kuwaiti citizens whereas their own husbands and children were prevented from enjoying similar rights?

In April 1991 the Association of Kuwaiti Women Married to Non-Kuwaitis was formed under the presidency of Dr Badria al-Awadi, a Kuwaiti lawyer. For over a year, the association used the premises of the Environmental Protection Society (EPS) as its headquarters until they were told by the all-male society's board to look for new premises. The EPS provided a gathering-place where more than 200 women met every week to talk about their own problems and to provide emotional and financial support for each other. On 25 January 1992, 13 members met with the Prime Minister, Sheikh Saad al-Abdullah Al Sabah, demanding that their husbands and children be given the legal right to live and work in Kuwait. Promises were made but no action was taken, and the situation of Kuwaiti women married to non-Kuwaitis remains unchanged. In an interview with the Kuwaiti newspaper *al-Watan* on 2 March 1993, one woman said, 'The authorities have put our men out of work, deported some of them, and made our children feel inferior in a society in which they were born . . . And, in spite of all their promises for the last two years our problems are still unresolved.'

On 1 February 1993 the women put their grievances in writing to the National Assembly. They demanded: permanent residence for their husbands and children; government housing; education and work for their children; free medical care; and a family allowance. The demands were put to the Assembly's Grievances Committee, together with the demand for political rights submitted earlier by a group of Kuwaiti women. In 1992, during the election campaign for the National Assembly, more than 100 Kuwaiti women had staged protests at polling stations calling for women's suffrage. At that time, most of the candidates spoke in favour of women's suffrage and called for increased democratic rights. But later, the new deputies saw no urgency or need to debate the issue in the house. The argument that Islam has given women their full rights in well-defined gender roles was once again revived.

In November 1992, at a seminar on 'Women's Political Rights in Islam' organized by the Islamic Heritage Society, Ahmad Baqer, the National Assembly Secretary-General, stated that women are more emotional and weaker than men and that 'God has kept women away from participating in political matters, because they only possess specific capabilities and instincts inadequate for the political field.'[2] Al-Duwaila, a senior member of the National Assembly, called upon women to reassess their priorities with a view to putting a much higher emphasis on domestic duties. 'Women in Kuwait', he said, 'have neglected their basic roles, which are to take care of and look after their families.' He added that the issue of women's suffrage could only be ruled on by the Ministry of Awqaf and Islamic Affairs.[3]

The women's societies failed to organize women or to launch a campaign to secure women's rights. They returned to their previous preoccupations, with their same leaders and their same members. Only recently, in February 1993, did the WCSS adopt the issue of Kuwaiti women married to non-Kuwaitis and invite those women concerned to use its premises to hold meetings.

The lack of co-ordination and solidarity among Kuwaiti women has undermined all attempts to tackle the serious problems faced by women in their everyday lives. Women are still being prosecuted for committing so-called 'moral crimes'. They have no legal protection against any form of abuse within marriage and no citizenship rights similar to those of Kuwaiti men, and face constant discrimination at work. It is therefore vital that Kuwaiti women unite across class boundaries if changes in women's status are to be achieved. Given the uncompromising stance of male society, it is clear that the challenge facing Kuwaiti women is daunting and changes will be slow to achieve. But, in the face of such a challenge, unity is a step forward for women towards the remaking of their own history and the realization of a better future.

Notes

Preface

1. Colette Dowling, *The Cinderella Complex*, London 1982.

Introduction

1. Halim Barakat, 'The Arab Family and the Challenge of Social Transformation', in Elizabeth Fernea (ed.), *Women and the Family in the Middle East,* Austin 1985, p. 37.

2. Deniz Kandiyoti, 'Urban Change and Women's Roles: An Overview and Evaluation', in Helen Rivlin and Katherine Helmer, *The Changing Middle Eastern City,* New York 1980.

3. Tawfic Farrah, 'Inculcating Supportive Attitudes in an Emerging State: the Case of Kuwait', *Journal of South Asian and Middle Eastern Studies,* 1979, p. 51.

4. Fahd al-Thakeb, 'Family–Kin Relationships in Contemporary Kuwait Society', *Annals of the Faculty of Arts,* Vol. 3, 1982.

5. Muhammad Rumaihi, *Beyond Oil,* London 1986.

Chapter 1

1. Ahmad Anani and Ken Willington, *The Early History of the Gulf Arabs,* London 1986, p. 33.

2. The desert route was of special importance for trading purposes. Caravans carrying goods and sometimes passengers from South Arabia to Aleppo in Syria were unsafe in the desert. Tribes were thus paid to secure the safety of the caravan routes.

3. Louise E. Sweet, 'Camel Raiding of North Arabian Bedouin: A Mechanism of Ecological Adaptation', in Louise E. Sweet (ed.), *Peoples and Cultures of the Middle East,* New York 1970, p. 271.

4. See Jacqueline Ismael, *Kuwait: Social Change in Historical Perspective,* Syracuse, N.Y. 1982, p. 18.

5. J. E. Peterson, 'Tribes and Politics in Eastern Arabia', *The Middle East Journal,* Vol. 31, Summer 1977.

6. Harold Dickson, *The Arab of the Desert,* London 1983, p. 99.

7. Fred Halliday, 'Saudi Arabia: Bonanza and Repression', *New Left Review,* July–Aug. 1973, p. 6.

8. See: Yusuf bin Isa al-Qinae, *Safahat min Tarikh al-Kuwayt* (Pages from the History of Kuwait), Kuwait 1968; Abdul Aziz al-Rushaid, *Tarikh al-Kuwayt*

(The History of Kuwait), Beirut 1971; and Sayf Marzook al-Shamlan, *Min Tarikh al-Kuwayt* (From the History of Kuwait), Kuwait 1986. See also the excellent work of Ahmad M. Abu Hakima, *History of Eastern Arabia, 1750–1800,* Beirut 1965.

9. Abu Hakima, *History of Eastern Arabia* . . . , p. 96.

10. Clifford W. Hawks, *The Dhow*, Lausanne 1977, p. 42.

11. Abu Hakima, *The Modern History of Kuwait, 1750–1965,* London 1983, p. 102.

12. Ibid., p. 103.

13. For a detailed account of the pearling industry in the Gulf, see the excellent work of Sayf Marzook al-Shamlan, *Tarikh al-Ghaus ala al-Lulu fi al-Kuwayt wa al-Khalij al-Arabi* (History of Pearling in Kuwait and the Arabian Gulf), Kuwait 1975; and Richard Le Baron Bowen, 'Pearl Fisheries of the Persian Gulf', *The Middle East Journal*, no. 2, Spring 1951.

14. Ismael, *Kuwait: Social Change* . . . , p. 61.

15. Ibid., p. 63.

16. Ibid., p. 61.

17. Alain Villiers, 'Some Aspects of the Arab Dhow Trade', in Sweet (ed.), *Peoples and Cultures of the Middle East.*

18. The India Office Record, London, IOR R/15/5/196.

19. Villiers, 'Aspects of the Arab Dhow Trade', p. 162.

20. Peterson, 'Tribes and Politics . . .' , p. 234.

21. Hassan al-Ebraheem, *Kuwait: A Political Study*, Kuwait 1975, p. 51.

22. Ibid., pp. 51-7.

23. Ibid., p. 46.

24. See al-Shamlan, *History of Pearling* . . . , pp. 67–71.

25. Naseer H. Aruri, 'Politics in Kuwait', in Jacob Landau (ed.), *Man, State and Society in the Contemporary Middle East,* London 1972, p. 80.

26. Huda Nashif, *Pre-School Education in the Arab World,* London 1985, p. 19.

27. Public Record Office, London, FO 371/21832.

28. Public Record Office, London, FO 371/21833.

29. Khalid al-Adsani, *Nisf Am lil Hukm al-Niyabi fi al-Kuwayt* (A Half-Year of Parliamentary Rule in Kuwait), Kuwait 1947.

30. The India Office Record, London, IOR R/15/1/548.

31. Stephen Gardiner, *Kuwait: The Making of a City*, London 1983, p. 53.

32. Public Record Office, London, FO 371/104330.

33. Hassan al-Ebraheem, *Kuwait and the Gulf,* London 1984, p. 95.

34. Hassan Hamoud, 'Kuwait', in John Dixon (ed.), *Social Welfare in the Middle East*, London 1987, p. 124.

35. Public Record Office, London, FO 371/109810.

36. Ibid.

37. Ismael, *Kuwait: Social Change . . .* , p. 83.

38. *Professional associations*: Engineers Society, Lawyers Society, Teachers Society, Kuwait Medical Association, Graduates Society, Journalists Association, Writers Society, Sociologists Society, Economists Society, Geographic Society, Kuwaiti Aircraft Engineers and Pilots Association, Agricultural Engineers Society, Environmental Protection Society, Kuwaiti Society of Accountants and Auditors, Pharmaceutical Association, Dentists Society, Shareholders Society, Nurses Society, Kuwaiti Chemical Society, Heart Society, Transplant Society.
Welfare and charitable associations: Centre for Child Evaluation and Teaching, Society for the Handicapped, Kuwait Society for the Development of Arab Children, Safety Society, al-Najat Charitable Society, Sheikh Abdullah al-Nouri Charitable Association, Anti-Smoking and Cancer Prevention Society, Kuwait Red Crescent Society, Charity Fund Society, Society for the Blind.
Educational societies: Science Club, Computer Society, Sultan Educational Society, South and Arabian Gulf Society, Society for the Advanced Education of Palestinian Students.
Recreational/Hobbies societies: Cine-Club, Kuwait Amateur Radio Society, Chess Society, Kuwait Club for the Deaf.
Religious (Islamic) societies: Social Reform Society, Islamic Heritage Society, Cultural and Social Society.
Women's societies: Women's Cultural and Social Society, Bayader al-Salam, Girls Club, Islamic Care Society.
Music and drama societies: Dramatic Society of the Arabian Gulf, Kuwait Artists Society, Kuwaiti Drama Society, Folklore & Drama Society, Arab Drama Society, Kuwait Arts Society.

39. In March 1993, 1 Kuwaiti dinar (KD1) was worth approximately £2.00.

40. The data are based on a questionnaire distributed to 52 voluntary organizations in Kuwait.

41. Kuwait Ministry of Planning, Central Statistical Office, *Annual Statistical Abstract,* 1988.

42. Robert Landen, quoted in Ahmad Abdullah Saad Baz, 'Political Elites and Political Development in Kuwait', unpub. PhD dissertation, George Washington University 1981, p. 207.

43. Jill Crystal, 'Patterns of State-Building in the Arabian Gulf: Kuwait and Qatar', unpub. PhD dissertation, Harvard University 1986, p. 208.

44. Ibid., p. 209.

45. J. E. Peterson, 'The Arab Gulf States', *The Washington Papers,* no. 131, p. 41.

46. Crystal, 'Patterns of State-Building . . . ', p. 226.

47. Ibid., p. 237.

Notes

Chapter 2

1. Zahra Freeth, *Kuwait was my Home,* London 1956, p. 83.

2. J.G. Lorimer, *Gazetteer of the Persian Gulf,* Vol. 2B, quoted in Royal Scottish Museum, *The Evolving Culture of Kuwait,* Edinburgh 1985, p. 30.

3. Yusuf bin Isa al-Qinaie, *Safahat min Tarikh al-Kuwayt* (Pages from the History of Kuwait), Kuwait 1968, p. 66.

4. Freeth, *Kuwait was my Home*, p. 84.

5. See Nouria al-Sadani, *Tarikh al-Mar'a al-Kuwaytia* (The History of Kuwaiti Women), Kuwait 1972, pp. 49–50.

6. Ina Robertson, 'Arab Women of Al-Kuwait', in Henry Field (ed.), *Folklore of South Western Asia,* Chicago 1940, p. 163.

7. Freeth, *Kuwait was my Home*, p. 84.

8. Robertson, 'Arab Women of Al-Kuwait', p. 164.

9. Al-Qinaie, *Pages from the History of Kuwait,* p. 78.

10. Najat Sultan, 'The Professional Kuwaiti Woman *vis-à-vis* the Situation of Women', paper presented to the AAUG Ninth Annual Convention, New York, 1–3 Oct. 1976, p. 4.

11. Al-Qinaie, *Pages from the History of Kuwait*, p. 78.

12. Ibid., p. 79.

13. Robertson, 'Arab Women of Al-Kuwait', p. 161.

14. Freeth, *Kuwait was my Home*, p. 88.

15. Al-Sadani, *History of Kuwaiti Women,* pp. 49–55.

16. Al-Qinaie, *Pages from the History of Kuwait*, p. 78.

17. Ibid., p. 80.

18. Dalal al-Zaban, 'The Kuwaiti Woman and her Role in the Labour Force', paper presented to the third Regional Conference on Women in the Arabian Gulf, Abu Dhabi, 24–27 March 1984.

19. Huda Nashif, *Pre-School Education in the Arab World,* London 1985, pp. 22–3.

20. Ibid., p. 23.

21. Robertson, 'Arab Women of Al-Kuwait', p. 165.

22. Al-Qinaie, *Pages from the History of Kuwait*, p. 80.

23. Ibid.

24. Ioan Lewis, *Ecstatic Religion,* Harmondsworth 1971, p. 72.

25. Robertson, 'Arab Women of Al-Kuwait', p. 165.

26. Lewis, *Ecstatic Religion*, p. 27.

27. Al-Sadani, *History of Kuwaiti Women*, p. 65.

28. See Lewis, *Ecstatic Religion*.

29. See Muhammad Hassan Abdullah, *al-Haraka al-Adabiya fi al-Kuwayt* (The Cultural Movement in Kuwait), Kuwait 1973.

30. *Al-Ba'tha,* March 1950.

31. See, for example, ibid., 1950.

32. Ibid., Feb. 1954.
33. Nancy F. Cott, 'Feminist Theory and Feminist Movements: The Past Before Us', in Juliet Mitchell and Ann Oakley (eds), *What is Feminism*, Oxford 1986, p. 50.
34. *Al-Ba'tha,* Feb. 1954.
35. Ibid., April 1954.
36. *Al-Sha'b,* 15 Jan. 1959.
37. *Al-Ba'tha*, 1950.
38. *Al-Sha'b*, 20 March 1958.
39. *Al-Ba'tha*, Feb. 1948.
40. Freeth, *Kuwait was my Home*, p. 84.
41. *Al-Sha'b*, 1 Jan. 1959.
42. Ibid.
43. Ibid., 13 March 1958.
44. See, for example, the debate in *al-Ba'tha,* March 1950.
45. *Al-Sha'b,* 1 Jan. 1959.
46. Ibid., 13 March 1958.
47. *Al-Iman,* May 1953.
48. See *al-Ba'tha*, July 1954.
49. Abdullah, *The Cultural Movement . . .*, p. 90.
50. Zahra Freeth, *A New Look at Kuwait*, London 1972, p. 35.
51. See *al-Sha'b*, 27 Feb. 1958.
52. Sultan, 'The Professional Kuwaiti Woman . . .', p. 17.
53. See Kamla Nath, 'Education and Employment Among Kuwaiti Women', in Lois Beck and Nikki Keddie (eds), *Women in the Muslim World*, Cambridge, Mass. 1978, pp. 172–88.
54. *Al-Hadaf,* Nov. 1961.
55. Ibid., 21 Oct. 1961.
56. *Al-Talia*, 23 Dec. 1964.
57. *Al-Hadaf,* 21 Oct. 1961.
58. *Al-Iman*, Jan. 1953.
59. Freeth, *A New Look at Kuwait*, p. 37.
60. See Sultan, 'The Professional Kuwaiti Woman . . .'.
61. See *Dunia al-Uruba*, 2 Feb. 1963.
62. Henrietta Moore, *Feminism and Anthropology*, Cambridge 1988, p. 129.
63. Kuwait Ministry of Planning, *The First Five Year Development Plan 1967/68–1971/72*, p. 132.
64. Ibid., p. 133.
65. Kuwait Ministry of Planning, *The Five Year Development Plan 1985/86–1989/90*, Part I, p. 45.
66. Maxine Molyneux, 'Socialist Societies Old and New: Progress towards Women's Emancipation', *Feminist Review*, Summer 1981, pp. 14–15.

Chapter 3

1. *Al-Iman*, April 1955.
2. *Al-Hadaf,* 4 April 1962.
3. Ibid., 26 Sept. 1962.
4. Ibid., 1 Aug. 1962.
5. *The Progress of Kuwaiti Women for 11 Years through the Arab Women's Development Society,* AWDS Publications, Kuwait n.d., pp. 113–14.
6. Najat Sultan, 'The Professional Kuwaiti Woman *vis-à-vis* the Situation of Women', paper presented to the AAUG Ninth Annual Convention, New York, 1–3 Oct. 1976, p. 18.
7. *Progress of Kuwaiti Women for 11 Years* . . . , p. 114.
8. Kuwait Ministry of Social Affairs and Labour, Dept of Public Welfare Societies, *Minutes of the First Meeting with the WCSS Board,* Aug. 1967.
9. Kuwait Ministry of Public Works, *Report on the Building Cost of the WCSS Headquarters*, 22 June 1980.
10. Article 9, WCSS constitution.
11. In the 1970s, article 2 of the constitution was amended to allow students to become members.
12. *Al-Nahda*, 25 Jan. 1969.
13. Quoted in *Kuwaiti Women in the Past and Present*, AWDS Publications, Kuwait n.d., p. 91.
14. *Mar'at al-Umma,* 15 Dec. 1971.
15. *Al-Kuwayt,* April 1964.
16. *Kuwaiti Women in the Past and Present,* p. 90.
17. *Al-Nahda*, 30 Dec. 1978.
18. Henrietta Moore, *Feminism and Anthropology,* Cambridge 1988, p. 129.
19. See 'The First Regional Conference on Women in the Arabian Gulf', *Journal of the Gulf and Arabian Peninsula*, July 1975, pp. 225–9.
20. *Progress of Kuwaiti Women for 11 Years* . . . , pp. 18–24.
21. Ibid., p. 29.
22. For a full text of the lecture, see ibid., pp. 29–33.
23. Ibid., p. 32.
24. Ibid., pp. 36–42.
25. Ibid., p. 64.
26. Ibid., pp. 57–62.
27. Nouria al-Sadani, *Tarikh al-Mar'a al-Kuwaytia* (The History of Kuwaiti Women), Kuwait 1980, Vol. II, pp. 347–51.
28. *Kuwait Times,* 25 Dec. 1973.
29. Ibid., 2 Dec. 1973.
30. Al-Sadani, *History of Kuwaiti Women*, p. 284.
31. Ibid., p. 268.
32. Ibid., p. 247.

33. Ibid., p. 156.
34. Ibid., p. 152.
35. Ibid., p. 157.
36. Ibid., p. 113.
37. Ibid., p. 247.
38. Ibid., p. 164.
39. Ibid., pp. 339–45.
40. Ibid.
41. See *al-Siyassah,* 1 Dec. 1973.
42. *Progress of Kuwaiti Women for 11 Years . . .* , pp. 97–100.
43. Ibid., pp. 101–7.
44. Al-Sadani, *History of Kuwaiti Women*, p. 509.
45. *Al-Ra'y al-Amm,* 12 Dec. 1973.
46. The KWU's objectives were: (i) to look after the interests of societies which were members; (ii) to help the societies financially; (iii) to help in the formulation of any projects that would serve the community; (iv) to co-ordinate the societies with regard to conferences and seminars; (v) to set up projects in the fields of family planning, childcare and the care of the elderly; (vi) to increase public awareness of the importance of the family and support for women's activities; and (vii) to serve the interests of Kuwaiti women.
47. Al-Sadani, *History of Kuwaiti Women,* pp. 579–86.
48. Article 2, Girls Club constitution.
49. Al-Sadani, *History of Kuwaiti Women,* p. 345.
50. Nouria Al-Sadani, *al-Haraka al-Nisaiya al-Arabia fi al-Qarn al-Isrun* (The Arab Women's Movement in the Twentieth Century), Kuwait 1982, p. 72.
51. See, for example, Marian Simms, 'Conservative Feminism in Australia: A Case Study of Feminist Ideology', *Women's Studies International Quarterly,* 1979, Vol. 2, pp. 305–18.

Chapter 4

1. See Yvonne Haddad, 'Islamic Awakening in Egypt', *Arab Studies Quarterly,* Vol. 9, Summer 1987, pp. 234–59.
2. Ibid., p. 237.
3. Nouria al-Sadani, *Tarikh al-Mar'a al-Kuwaytia* (The History of Kuwaiti Women), Kuwait 1980, Vol. II, p. 172.
4. *Al-Qabas,* 8 Jan. 1988.
5. Michael Gilsenan, *Saint and Sufi in Modern Egypt,* Oxford 1973, p. 68.
6. Note that the *tariqa* also implies a Sufi order and usually bears a name derived from that of the founder of the order; see Jean-Louis Michon, 'The Spiritual Practices of Sufism', in Seyyed H. Nasr (ed.), *Islamic Spirituality,* London 1987, p. 270.
7. Sufism has attracted great interest among Western scholars. It is beyond

the scope of this study to give a detailed account of the Sufi tradition in Islam. For a full treatment, see: Nasr, *Islamic Spirituality;* John A. Subnan, *Sufism, Its Saints and Shrines,* New York 1970; Nikki R. Keddie (ed.), *Scholars, Saints and Sufis,* Berkeley 1972; and J. Spencer Trimingham, *The Sufi Orders in Islam,* Oxford 1971.

8. Interview with Bayader member, Kuwait, 2 Feb. 1988.

9. Michon, 'Spiritual Practices of Sufism', in Nasr (ed.), *Islamic Spirituality,* p. 273.

10. Bassama al-Musallam, 'Women's Education in Kuwait and its Effect on Future Expectations: An Ethnography of a Girls' Sex-Segregated Secondary School', unpub. PhD dissertation, New York University 1984, p. 90.

11. Ibid.

12. The founder of the Salafiya movement in Kuwait, Abdul Rahman Abdul-Khaleq, has published two books: *The Sufi Doctrine in the Light of the Quran and Sunnah,* Kuwait 1986; and *Sufi Scandals,* Kuwait 1988.

13. *Ya Rab* (O God), Bayader Publications, Kuwait 1987, pp. 11–13.

14. Ibid.

15. In Sufism, *nafs* means the lower self. Milson explains that 'it is the *nafs* that commands evil. The Prophet used to seek refuge in God from the *nafs*. . . *Nafs* is an opposite to God. The soul is the substratum of blameworthy qualities. The spirit [*ruh*] is the mine of good and the soul is the mine of evil.' See Menahem Milson, *A Sufi Rule for Novices,* Cambridge, Mass. 1975, p. 44.

16. Trimingham, *The Sufi Orders* . . . , p. 199.

17. See Yvonne Haddad, 'Traditional Affirmations Concerning the Role of Women as Found in Contemporary Arab Islamic Literature', in Janet Smith (ed.), *Women in Contemporary Muslim Societies,* London 1980, p. 64.

18. Bayader al-Salam, *Zakat Committee*, Kuwait 1987.

19. *A Brief Outline of the History and Activities of the Islamic Care Society,* ICS Publications, Kuwait n.d., p. 15.

20. Ibid., p. 16.

21. Ibid., p. 18.

22. See Kuwait Ministry of Awqaf and Islamic Affairs, *An Introduction to Dar al-Quran,* Kuwait 1985, p. 15.

23. *Brief Outline of the . . . Islamic Care Society*, pp. 26–7.

24. Nadia Hijab, *Womanpower,* Cambridge 1988, p. 52.

25. See Robert Michels, *Political Parties,* New York 1968.

26. In 1988, of the 93 registered members, there were 26 housewives, 4 students and 63 working women. Of the working women, 41 were teachers, 11 were in administrative jobs and 5 were secretaries. The others were lawyers, dentists and journalists. Of the 9 board members, 6 were housewives with secondary diplomas, 2 were teachers and 1 was a dentist.

27. *Brief Outline of the . . . Islamic Care Society,* p. 13.

28. Ibid.

29. *Al-Kauter,* Feb. 1986. A monthly magazine published by the ICS, *al-Kauter* is the name of a river in Paradise.

30. Michels, *Political Parties*, p. 83.

31. Lulua al-Qitami, 'The *Status Quo* of Women in Kuwait', paper delivered during the Kuwaiti Cultural Week held in Algeria, 31 March–7 April 1986.

32. See the bylaws of the Women's Co-ordinating Committee for the Gulf and Arabian Peninsula, 1984.

33. *Mar'at al-Umma,* 15 Dec. 1971.

34. Patricia Caplan, *Class and Gender in India,* London 1985, p. 167.

35. What Bourdieu refers to as *l'habitus*: see Pierre Bourdieu, *La Distinction,* Paris 1979.

36. See, for example: Claire Robertson and Iris Berger, *Women and Class in Africa,* New York 1986; and Caplan, *Class and Gender in India.*

Chapter 5

1. See, for example: Dana al-Fulaij and Ikbal al-Mussallam, *al-Islam wa al-Mar'a* (Islam and Women), Kuwait 1984; Sheikh Ahmad al-Qatan, *al-Mar'a fi al-Islam* (Women in Islam), Kuwait 1987; Anwar al-Jindi, *al-Ma'ra al-Muslima fi Wajh al-Tahdidad* (The Muslim Woman in the Face of Provocation), Kuwait 1983; Abdullah bin Jarallah bin Ibrahim al-Jarallah, *Mas'uliyat al-Mar'a al-Muslima* (The Responsibilities of the Muslim Woman), Kuwait 1987; Ahmad bin Abdul-Aziz al-Hassan, *Ra'y al-Shari'a fi al-Mar'a* (The Shari'a's View on Women), Kuwait 1987; Teiba al-Yahia, *Wajibat al-Mar'a al-Muslima* (The Duties of the Muslim Woman), Kuwait 1981; Badria al-Azaz and Sheikha al-Hamad, *al-Mar'a Auda ila al-Asala* (Women and the Return to Authenticity), Kuwait n. d.; Sheikh Abdul Aziz bin Baz and Sheikh Muhammad al-Othaimeen, *Risalatan fi al-Hijab* (Two Letters on the Veil), Saudi Arabia 1987; Wael al-Hassawi, *al-Da'wa al-Islamiya fi al-Kuwayt* (Islamic Preaching in Kuwait), Kuwait 1985; and Abdullah al-Nafissi, *al-Amal al-Nisai fi al-Kuwayt: al-Waqa' wa al-Murtaja* (Women's Activity in Kuwait: The Actual and the Expected), Kuwait 1984.

2. Fatima Mernissi, 'Democracy as Moral Disintegration: The Contradiction Between Religious Belief and Citizenship as a Manifestation of the Ahistoricity of the Arab Identity', in Nadia Toubia (ed.), *Women of the Arab World,* London 1988, p. 37.

3. Al-Hassawi, *Islamic Preaching in Kuwait,* pp. 17–19.

4. Ibid.

5. Al-Nafissi, *Women's Activity in Kuwait . . . ,* pp. 7–8.

6. Ibid., p. 11.

7. Al-Qatan, *Women in Islam,* p. 44.

8. Fatima Mernissi, *Beyond the Veil,* London 1985, p. 44.

9. Al-Qatan, *Women in Islam,* p. 20.
10. *The Holy Quran,* Verse 34, Sura IV.
11. Al-Qatan, *Women in Islam,* p. 144.
12. *The Holy Quran,* Verse 34, Sura IV.
13. Sheikh Muhammad Iman bin Ali al-Jami, *Nizam al-Usra fi al-Islam* (The Family System in Islam), Kuwait 1986, p. 34.
14. See, for example, Penelope Brown and L. J. Jordanova, 'Oppressive Dichotomies: The Nature/Culture Debate', in Cambridge Women's Studies Group (ed.), *Women in Society, Interdisciplinary Essays,* London 1981, pp. 224–41.
15. Jane Caplan, 'Introduction to Female Sexuality in Fascist Ideology', *Feminist Review,* 1979, pp. 59–66.
16. *Manbar al-Taliba,* March 1983.
17. See, for example, al-Fulaij and al-Mussallam, *Islam and Women.*
18. Al-Yahia, *Duties of the Muslim Woman.*
19. Ibid., pp. 13–14.
20. *Manbar al-Taliba,* March 1982.
21. Seyyed H. Nasr (ed.), *Islamic Spirituality,* London 1987, p. xvi.
22. Ibid., p. xv.
23. Saadia Khawar Khan Chishti, 'Female Spirituality in Islam', in Nasr (ed.), *Islamic Spirituality,* p. 215.
24. Ibid., p. 213.
25. Ursula King, *Women and Spirituality: Voices of Protest and Promise,* London 1989, pp. 112–13.
26. *Manbar al-Taliba,* March 1983.
27. King, *Women and Spirituality . . . ,* p. 110.
28. Margaret Smith, *Rabi'a the Mystic,* Amsterdam 1974, p. 175.
29. Quoted in Fatna A. Sabbah, *Woman in the Muslim Unconscious,* Oxford 1984, p. 116.
30. ICS, *Report on the Third Regional Women's Conference,* Kuwait 1984.
31. Ibid.
32. ICS, *al-Suq al-Khairi al-Thani* (The Second Charity Bazaar), Kuwait 1987, p. 9.
33. *The Holy Quran,* Verse 59, Sura XXXIII.
34. *The Middle East,* May 1978.
35. *Women and Development in the Eighties,* WCSS Publications, Kuwait 1982, p. 2.
36. Lulua al-Qitami, 'The Kuwaiti Woman: The Present and the Expected', paper presented at the UN World Conference on Women, Nairobi 1985.
37. Quoted in J. E. Peterson, 'The Arab Gulf States', *The Washington Papers,* no. 131, p. 58.
38. Nouria al-Sadani, *al-Masira al-Tarikhiya lil Huquq Siyasiya lil Mar'a al-*

Kuwaytia fi Fatra ma-bain 1971–1982 (The History of the Kuwaiti Women's Movement for Political Rights, 1971–1982), Kuwait 1983, p. 162.

39. Quoted in al-Qatan, *Women in Islam,* pp. 149–50.

40. *Al-Watan,* 10 Feb. 1982.

41. Peterson, 'Arab Gulf States', p. 59.

42. *The Middle East,* Oct. 1985.

43. WCSS, 'Project for a Model Nursery in the State of Kuwait', Feb. 1979, p. 3.

44. Kuwait Ministry of Planning, *The Five Year Development Plan 1985/86–1989/90,* Part I, p. 50.

45. Ibid., p. 56.

Conclusion

1. Hannah Papanek, 'Family Status Production: The ''Work'' and ''Non Work'' of Women', *Signs,* Vol. 4, 1979, pp. 775–81.

2. Ann Whitehead, 'Women's Solidarity and Divisions Among Women', *IDS Bulletin,* Vol. 15, 1984, p. 8.

Postscript

1. The Public Authority for Civil Information (PACI), Kuwait, 1993.

2. *Arab Times*, 15 Nov. 1992.

3. Ibid., 11–12 March 1993.

Bibliography

Books and Articles in English

Abu Hakima, Ahmad M. *History of Eastern Arabia, 1750–1800: The Rise and Development of Bahrain and Kuwait*. Beirut: Khayats, 1965.

———*The Modern History of Kuwait, 1750–1965*. London: Luzac & Co., 1983.

Afshar, Haleh. 'Khomeini's Teachings and their Implications for Women'. *Feminist Review*, 12 (1982): 59–72.

———(ed.) *Women, State and Ideology*. London: MacMillan, 1987.

Ahmad, Leila. 'Feminism and Feminist Movements in the Middle East, A Preliminary Exploration: Turkey, Egypt, Algeria, People's Democratic Republic of Yemen'. In Azizah al-Hibri (ed.), *Women and Islam*, Oxford: Pergamon Press, 1982.

al-Ebraheem, Hassan. *Kuwait: A Political Study*. Kuwait: Kuwait University Press, 1975.

———*Kuwait and the Gulf*. London: Croom Helm, 1984.

al-Hibri, Azizah (ed.). *Women and Islam*. Oxford: Pergamon Press, 1982.

al-Misnad, Sheikha. *The Development of Modern Education in the Gulf*. London: Ithaca Press, 1985.

al-Musallam, Bassama. 'Women's Education in Kuwait and its Effect on Future Expectations: An Ethnography of a Girls' Sex-Segregated Secondary School' (unpub. PhD dissertation, New York University, 1984).

al-Qitami, Lulua. 'The Kuwaiti Woman: The Present and the Expected' (paper presented at the UN International Women's Conference, Nairobi, July 1985).

al-Thakeb, Fahad. 'Family–Kin Relationships in Contemporary Kuwait Society'. *Annals of the Faculty of Arts*, 3 (1982).

Altorki, Soraya. *Women in Saudi Arabia*. New York: Columbia University Press, 1986.

Anani, Ahmad and Willington, Ken. *The Early History of the Gulf Arabs*. London: Longman, 1986.

Aruri, H. Naseer. 'Politics in Kuwait'. In Jacob Landau (ed.), *Man, State and Society in the Contemporary Middle East,* London: Pall Mall Press, 1972.

Barakat, Halim. 'The Arab Family and the Challenge of Social Transformation'. In Elizabeth Fernea (ed.), *Women and the Family in the Middle East*, Austin: University of Texas Press, 1985.

Baz, Ahmad Abdullah Saad. 'Political Elites and Political Development in Kuwait' (unpub. PhD dissertation, George Washington University, 1981).

Bibliography

Beck, Lois and Keddie, Nikki (eds). *Women in the Muslim World.* Cambridge, Mass.: Harvard University Press, 1978.

Bill, James. 'Resurgent Islam in the Persian Gulf'. *Foreign Affairs,* 63 (Fall 1984): 108–27.

Bouhdiba, Abdelwahab. *Sexuality in Islam.* London: Routledge & Kegan Paul, 1985.

Bourdieu, Pierre. *La Distinction.* Paris: Editions de Minuit, 1979.

Bowen, Richard Le Baron. 'Pearl Fisheries of the Persian Gulf'. *The Middle East Journal,* 2 (Spring 1951): 161–80.

Brown, Penelope and Jordanova, L.J., 'Oppressive Dichotomies: The Nature/Culture Debate'. In Cambridge Women's Studies Group (ed.), *Women in Society, Interdisciplinary Essays,* London: Virago, 1981.

Caplan, Jane. 'Introduction to Female Sexuality in Fascist Ideology'. *Feminist Review*, 1 (1979): 59–66.

Caplan, Patricia. *Class and Gender in India: Women and their Organisations in a South Indian City.* London: Tavistock, 1985.

Caplan, Patricia and Bujra, Janet (eds). *Women United, Women Divided.* London: Tavistock, 1978.

Carter, J.R.L. *Merchant Families of Kuwait.* London: Scorpion Books, 1984.

Chishti, Saadia Khawar Khan. 'Female Spirituality in Islam'. In Seyyed H. Nasr (ed.), *Islamic Spirituality*, London: Routledge & Kegan Paul, 1987.

Cott, Nancy F. 'Feminist Theory and Feminist Movements: The Past Before Us'. In Juliet Mitchell and Ann Oakley (eds), *What is Feminism,* Oxford: Basil Blackwell, 1986.

Crystal, Jill. 'Patterns of State-Building in the Arabian Gulf: Kuwait and Qatar' (unpub. PhD dissertation, Harvard University, 1986).

Dickson, Harold. *The Arab of the Desert.* London: George Allen & Unwin, 1983.

Dickson, Violet. *Forty Years in Kuwait.* London: George Allen & Unwin, 1971.

Divine, R. Donna. 'Unveiling the Mysteries of Islam: The Art of Studying Muslim Women'. *Journal of South Asian and Middle Eastern Studies*, 7 (1983): 3–19.

Dixon, John (ed.). *Social Welfare in the Middle East.* London: Croom Helm, 1987.

Dwyer, Daisy Hilse. *Images and Self-Images: Male and Female in Morocco.* New York: Columbia University Press, 1978.

Esposito, John. 'Women's Rights in Islam'. *Islamic Studies,* 14 (1975), 99–114.

———*Women in Muslim Family Law.* Syracuse, NY: Syracuse University Press, 1982.

Everett, Jana. *Women and Social Change in India.* New York: St Martin's Press, 1979.

Farrah, Tawfic. 'Inculcating Supportive Attitudes in an Emerging State: the Case of Kuwait'. *Journal of South Asian and Middle Eastern Studies*, 2 (1979).

Fernea, Elizabeth (ed.). *Women and the Family in the Middle East.* Austin: University of Texas Press, 1985.

Field, Michael. *The Merchants.* London: John Murray, 1984.

Freeth, Zahra. *Kuwait was my Home.* London: George Allen & Unwin, 1956.

———*A New Look at Kuwait.* London: George Allen & Unwin, 1972.

Gardiner, Stephen. *Kuwait: The Making of a City.* London: Longman, 1983.

Gilsenan, Michael. *Saint and Sufi in Modern Egypt.* Oxford: Clarendon Press, 1973.

Haddad, Yvonne. 'Islam, Women and Revolution in Twentieth-Century Arab Thought'. *The Muslim World,* LXXIV (July–Oct. 1984): 137–60.

———'Islamic Awakening in Egypt'. *Arab Studies Quarterly*, 9 (Summer 1987): 234–59.

Halliday, Fred. 'Saudi Arabia: Bonanza and Repression'. *New Left Review*, 80 (July–Aug. 1973): 3–26.

Hamoud, Hassan. 'Kuwait'. In John Dixon (ed.), *Social Welfare in the Middle East,* London: Croom Helm, 1987.

Hawks, Clifford W. *The Dhow.* Switzerland: Lausanne Edita, 1977.

Hijab, Nadia. *Womanpower: The Arab Debate on Women at Work.* Cambridge: Cambridge University Press, 1988.

Hindess, Barry. *Politics and Class Analysis.* Oxford: Basil Blackwell, 1987.

Hirschon, Renée (ed.). *Women and Property: Women as Property.* London: Croom Helm, 1984.

Hussain, Freda (ed.). *Muslim Women.* London: Croom Helm, 1984.

Ismael, Jacqueline. *Kuwait: Social Change in Historical Perspective.* Syracuse, N. Y.: Syracuse University Press, 1982.

Jayawardena, Kumari. *Feminism and Nationalism in the Third World.* London: Zed Press, 1986.

Kandiyoti, Deniz. 'Urban Change and Women's Roles: An Overview and Evaluation'. In Helen Rivlin and Katherine Helmer (eds), *The Changing Middle Eastern City,* New York: Center for Social Analysis and Program in Southwest Asian and North African Studies of the State University of New York, 1980.

Keddie, Nikki R. (ed.). *Scholars, Saints and Sufis.* Berkeley: University of California Press, 1972.

King, Ursula. *Women and Spirituality: Voices of Protest and Promise.* London: MacMillan, 1989.

Lewcock, Ronald and Freeth, Zahra. *Traditional Architecture in Kuwait and the Northern Gulf.* London: Art and Archeology Research Papers (AARP), 1978.

Lewis, Ioan. *Ecstatic Religion*. Harmondsworth: Penguin, 1971.

Liddle, Joanna and Joshi, Rama. *Daughters of Independence: Gender, Caste and Class in India*. London: Zed Press, 1986.

Lienhardt, Peter. 'The Authority of Shaykhs in the Gulf: An Essay in Nineteenth-Century History'. *Arabian Studies*, 2 (1975): 61–75.

Macciochi, Maria-Antonietta. 'Female Sexuality in Fascist Ideology'. *Feminist Review,* 1 (1979): 67–82.

Maher, Vanessa. *Women and Property in Morocco*. Cambridge: Cambridge University Press, 1974.

March, Kathryn and Taqqu, Rachelle. *Women's Informal Associations in Developing Countries: Catalysts for Change?* Boulder, Colo.: Westview Press, 1986.

Mernissi, Fatima. *Beyond the Veil.* London: Al Saqi Books, 1985.

———'Democracy as Moral Disintegration: The Contradiction Between Religious Belief and Citizenship as a Manifestation of the Ahistoricity of the Arab Identity'. In Nadia Toubia (ed.), *Women of the Arab World,* London: Zed Press, 1988.

Michels, Robert. *Political Parties: A Sociological Study of the Oligarchical Tendencies of Modern Democracy*. London: MacMillan, 1968.

Michon, Jean-Louis. 'The Spiritual Practices of Sufism'. In Seyyed H. Nasr (ed.), *Islamic Spirituality,* London: Routledge & Kegan Paul, 1987.

Mies, Maria. *Patriarchy and Accumulation on a World Scale: Women in the International Division of Labour*. London: Zed Press, 1986.

Milson, Menahem. *A Sufi Rule for Novices*. Cambridge, Mass.: Harvard University Press, 1975.

Minces, Juliette. *The House of Obedience: Women in Arab Society*. London: Zed Press, 1982.

Molyneux, Maxine. 'Socialist Societies Old and New: Progress towards Women's Emancipation'. *Feminist Review* (Summer 1981).

Monroe, Elizabeth. 'The Shaikhdom of Kuwait'. *International Affairs* (July 1954): 271–84.

Moore, Henrietta. *Feminism and Anthropology*. Cambridge: Polity Press, 1988.

Munson, Henry. 'Islamic Revivalism in Morocco and Tunisia'. *The Muslim World*, LXXVI (July–Oct. 1986): 203–18.

Nashif, Huda. *Pre-School Education in the Arab World*. London: Croom Helm, 1985.

Nasr, Seyyed H. (ed.). *Islamic Spirituality*. London: Routledge & Kegan Paul, 1987.

Nath, Kamla. 'Education and Employment Among Kuwaiti Women'. In Lois Beck and Nikki Keddie (eds), *Women in the Muslim World*, Cambridge, Mass.: Harvard University Press, 1978.

Papanek, Hannah. 'Purdah: Separate Worlds and Symbolic Shelter'. *Comparative Studies in Society and History*, 15 (1973): 289–325.

———'Family Status Production: The "Work" and "Non Work" of Women'. *Signs*, 4 (1984): 775–81.

Peterson, J.E. 'Tribes and Politics in Eastern Arabia'. *The Middle East Journal,* 31 (Summer 1977): 234–49.

———'The Arab Gulf States'. *The Washington Papers,* 131 (published with the Center for Strategic and International Studies, Washington, D.C., n.d.).

Rassam, Amal. 'Women and Domestic Power in Morocco'. *International Journal of Middle East Studies*, 12 (1980): 171–9.

Robertson, Claire and Berger, Iris (eds). *Women and Class in Africa*. New York: Africana Publishing Company, 1986.

Robertson, Ina. 'Arab Women of Al-Kuwait'. In Henry Field (ed.), *Folklore of South Western Asia*, Chicago: Field Museum of Natural History, 1940.

Rumaihi, Muhammad. *Beyond Oil*. London: Al Saqi Books, 1986.

Sabbah, Fatna A. *Woman in the Muslim Unconscious*. Oxford: Pergamon Press, 1984.

Scott, John. *The Upper Classes*. London: MacMillan, 1982.

Simms, Marian. 'Conservative Feminism in Australia: A Case Study of Feminist Ideology'. *Women's Studies International Quarterly,* 2 (1979): 305–18.

Smith, Janet (ed.). *Women in Contemporary Muslim Societies*. London: Associated University Presses, 1980.

Smith, Margaret. *Rabi'a the Mystic*. Amsterdam: Philo Press, 1974.

Springborg, Robert. *Family, Power and Politics in Egypt*. Philadelphia: University of Pennsylvania Press, 1982.

Subnan, John A. *Sufism, Its Saints and Shrines*. New York: Samuel Weiser, 1970.

Sultan, Najat. 'The Professional Kuwaiti Woman *vis-a-vis* the Situation of Women' (paper presented to the AAUG Ninth Annual Convention, New York, 1–3 Oct. 1976).

Sweet, Louise E. *Peoples and Cultures of the Middle East*, 2 vols. New York: The Natural History Press, 1970.

Tillion, Germaine. *The Republic of Cousins*. London: Al Saqi Books, 1983.

Toubia, Nadia (ed.). *Women of the Arab World*. London: Zed Press, 1988.

Trimingham, J. Spencer. *The Sufi Orders in Islam*. Oxford: Clarendon Press, 1971.

Villiers, Alain. 'Some Aspects of the Arab Dhow Trade'. In Louise E. Sweet (ed.), *Peoples and Cultures of the Middle East*, New York: The

Natural History Press, 1970.
Walby, Sylvia. *Patriarchy at Work.* Cambridge: Polity Press, 1986.
———*Theorizing Patriarchy.* Oxford: Basil Blackwell, 1990.
Whitehead, Ann. 'Women's Solidarity and Divisions Among Women'. *IDS Bulletin*, 15 (1984).
Wilson, Elizabeth. *Women and the Welfare State.* London: Tavistock, 1977.

Books and Articles in Arabic

Abdul Ghafoor, Badria. *Tatawur al-Ta'lim fi al-Kuwayt 1912–1972* (The Development of Education in Kuwait 1912–1972). Kuwait: Maktabat al-Falah, 1978.
Abdullah, Muhammad Hassan. *Al-Haraka al-Adabiya fi al-Kuwayt* (The Cultural Movement in Kuwait). Kuwait: Rabatat al-Udaba', 1973.
al-Adsani, Khalid. *Nisf Am lil Hukm al-Niyabi fi al-Kuwayt* (Half a Year of Parliamentary Rule in Kuwait). Kuwait: no pub., 1947.
al-Fulaij, Dana and al-Mussallam, Ikbal. *Al-Islam wa al-Mar'a* (Islam and Women). Kuwait: Dar al-Salafiya, 1984.
al-Hassawi, Wael. *Al-Da'wa al-Islamiya fi al-Kuwayt* (Islamic Preaching in Kuwait). Kuwait: Dar al-Salafiya, 1985.
al-Jasim, Najat Abdul Qadir. *Al-Tatawur al-Siyasi wa al-Iqtisadi lil Kuwayt bayn al-Harbayn, 1914–1939* (The Political and Economic Development of Kuwait Between the Two World Wars, 1914–1939). Cairo: al-Matbaah al-Faniya al-Haditha, 1973.
al-Mughni, Adel. *Al-Iqtisad al-Kuwayti al-Qadim* (The Traditional Kuwaiti Economy). Kuwait: no pub., 1977.
al-Nafissi, Abdullah. *Al-Amal al-Nisai fi al-Kuwayt: al-Waqa' wa al-Murtaja* (Women's Activity in Kuwait: The Actual and the Expected). Kuwait: Kuwait National Union of Students Publications, 1984.
al-Qatan, Ahmad. *Al-Mar'a fi al-Islam* (Women in Islam). Kuwait: Maktabat al-Sindus, 1987.
al-Qinaie, Yusuf bin Isa. *Safahat min Tarikh al-Kuwayt* (Pages from the History of Kuwait). Kuwait: Government Printing House, 1968.
al-Rushaid, Abdul Aziz. *Tarikh al-Kuwayt* (The History of Kuwait). Beirut: Manshurat Dar Matbaat al-Hayat, 1971.
al-Sadani, Nouria. *Tarikh al-Mar'a al-Kuwaytia* (The History of Kuwaiti Women), 2 vols. Kuwait: Matbaat Dar al-Siyassah, 1972 (Vol. I); 1980 (Vol. II).
———*Al-Haraka al-Nisaiya al-Arabia fi al-Qarn al-Isrun* (The Arab Women's Movement in the Twentieth Century). Kuwait: Matbaat Dar al-Siyassah, 1982.

———*Al-Masira al-Tarikhiya lil Huquq Siyasiya lil Mar'a al-Kuwaytia fi Fatra ma-bain 1971–1982* (The History of the Kuwaiti Women's Movement for Political Rights, 1971–1982). Kuwait: Matbaat Dar al-Siyassah, 1983.

al-Saleh, Mariam. *Safahat min Tatawur al-Tarikhi li Ta'lim al-Fatat fi al-Kuwayt* (Pages from the Historical Development of Girls' Education in Kuwait). Kuwait: Government Printing House, 1975.

al-Shamlan, Sayf Marzook. *Tarikh al-Ghaus ala al-Lulu fi al-Kuwayt wa al-Khalij al-Arabi* (History of Pearling in Kuwait and the Arabian Gulf). Kuwait: Government Printing Press, 1978.

———*Min Tarikh al-Kuwayt* (From the History of Kuwait). Kuwait: Manshurat Dar al-Salasel, 1986.

al-Yahia, Teiba. *Wajibat al-Mar'a al-Muslima* (The Duties of the Muslim Woman). Kuwait: Kuwait National Union of Students Publications, 1981.

Index